Reprinted, 1991, Ailsa, Inc.
ISBN: 0-940889-36-6

FLAGSTICK BOOKS

Edition of

OUT OF THE ROUGH

By
Joseph T. Shaw

Foreword by Archibald Gillies

Foreword

by

Archibald Gillies

I N 1940 -- just a few years after this charming book *Out of the Rough* was published -- the A.G. Spalding company invited Robert T. (Bobby) Jones, Jr. to record his by-then famous golf swing, using a new photographic process developed at the time by the Arthur D. Little Laboratories at M.I.T. in Cambridge. By taking rapid, multiple exposures on one film, the resulting, single photograph depicted the Jones swing in a dozen positions from start to finish.

Jones, writing about the experiment, noted that the picture demonstrated "in a very impressive fashion" the lack of movement of the head. In the backswing the head was "substantially immovable" -- so much so that while the legs, body, arms, and hands can be seen at once in successively new positions, the "face and the part of the hair" are almost as one throughout. In the downswing the head remains still at the beginning and moves "slightly backward and then definitely down as the ball was struck".

The hero of *Out of the Rough* Robert Hale, whose American innocence reminds us at once of the young Jimmy Stewart, encounters the same instruction from the old, dour Scot Sandy Macgregor -- to keep a steady head -- when he first arrives in Elie, Scotland, to learn the game of golf and, as we gradually discover, to learn the game of life as well. Our hero discovers that in his quest to master the ancient and honorable game he is in his words: "subjecting myself to a moral as well as a physical lesson".

And how many of us golfers have come to understand

and to cherish, to moan about and to laugh over the myriad ways in which the vagaries of our golf mirror, in some strange way, without strict analogy, the twists and turns, the dilemmas -- even the moral ones -- of our own lives. Of course we know that golf is "just a game", but we come to learn, as Robert Hale does, that how we play it, how we face up to its mental and physical challenges tells us much about ourselves.

Happily, and most importantly, in golf as in life there is always the chance of improvement, even of redemption. We can practice and take lessons -- from the Sandy Macgregors of the world if we are fortunate enough to find them -- and we can, in each new round of play, freshly anticipate possible improvement and, along the way, *learn* to appreciate, even if that improvement isn't realized, the incredible good luck of simply being alive.

Out of the Rough is set in the small town of Elie in Fife, Scotland. Elie sits on the Firth of Forth ten miles south of St. Andrews, and another ten miles directly across the Forth lie like a string of pearls the golfing towns of North Berwick, Muirfield, and Gullane. Golf was certainly played on the Elie linksland during the 16th and 17th centuries, but the Golf House Club was not officially formed until 1875. Elie in the late 1890s was home to many champion golfers including the great James Braid whose Scottish dictum that "anyone who didn't play golf was a crank" is fully worthy of *Out of the Rough's* Sandy Macgregor. Despite its past fame Elie today is a secret known only to the Scots, a small, wind-swept, astonishingly beautiful links that because of its almost-too-famous neighbor, the Old Course, has been spared the intrusion of the world's commercial glare. Elie is still the Elie of *Out of the Rough,* as Scottish and romantic as "Brigadoon".

I have been fortunate enough to be part of a group of friends who have played different links courses in Great

Britain a week a year for nearly twenty years now. I suppose in many ways I and my friends have had the same golfing education that Robert Hale had in *Out of the Rough*. Our trip to Elie was of course special because of the book. There it all was, the beauty of the village, the surrounding hills and farms, the way the course swept out of Elie through the next little town Earlsferry and down to the sea. We played the course twice on a clear day in a wind so bracing that a group of lady golfers we met decided not to venture out. Did we not also keep an innocent eye open for Robert Hale's "Jeannie" to appear?

Out of the Rough is dedicated to three Scottish friends who came from "across the Tweed", i.e. Scotland. The author Joseph Shaw was a Captain in the Army during the First World War with the Hoover Mission. This is when he got to know Scotland and Elie. Back in the States in 1926 he became the editor of a pulp magazine called the *Black Mask*. He had never read a pulp magazine before, and he had never been an editor -- of anything. Nevertheless, in ten years he transformed *Black Mask* into the leading detective magazine in the country and cultivated a new school of detective fiction, the so-called 'hardboiled detective story', that was to revolutionize the genre and make a unique contribution to American literature.

Ironically, in Shaw's own writing, it was in romance, the antithesis of the school of objective realism, that he succeeded. The testing of Robert Hale unfolds deliciously. I am confident that, right along with him, you will find yourself practicing his new strokes, reflecting on his new understandings and rooting for his happy outcome -- for "keeping a steady head" is only one of the lessons you will learn in this delightful golfing adventure. Nor would I be surprised if before too long you visited Elie.

OUT *of* THE ROUGH

BOOKS *by the* SAME AUTHOR

DANGER AHEAD
DERELICT
FUGITIVE

Can ye no say Ed'nbur-ra!

OUT *of* THE ROUGH

By
JOSEPH T. SHAW

Illustrated by
PAUL BROWN

WINDWARD HOUSE
NEW YORK

In Particular

To

SANDY ARMOUR, ALEX ROSS, TEDDIE GOW
Hard-shooting Musketeers from across
the Tweed who have canny understanding of this common affliction called golf.

Printed in U. S. A.

PRESS OF
BRAUNWORTH & CO., INC.
BOOK MANUFACTURERS
BROOKLYN, NEW YORK

LIST OF ILLUSTRATIONS

OUT *of* THE ROUGH

I

UNLIKE the famous Italian poet, I do not believe in exposing to the world one's intimate affairs if they pertain only to the heart.

Without further explanation, then—at Folothru one day I chanced to overhear Angelica emphatically state she would not think of marrying any man who could not make his round in the low eighties.

My own game was most unseemly—three figures and very lucky if I could subscribe a naught for the second. What to be done!

A night of bitter reflection yielded me finally an inspired idea.

Next day I put my things in order and booked an early passage to Southampton and London. I shared my confidence with no one . . .

From the foregoing, one may draw what conclusions one wishes. I have made no disclosure and I shall say no more on that subject—now.

As a matter of fact I am not at all sure my diary will ever surrender these notes which I am jotting as the Great Northern bears me steadily toward the

Tweed. It all depends upon the result of my enterprise. However, I shall now enter the statement that I am buoyed with hope. Surely such brightness of conception as is mine must bring suitable reward. We shall see. . . .

I change at Edinburgh, and a few hours later, the Scottish local takes me onward to the little village of Elie, on the Fife coast.

It's a quiet place, rarely if ever infested by tourists from across the water. That was a part of my shrewd plan.

At the only inn which Elie boasts, I find a room beyond my expectations—a great, square room with low ceiling crossed by fine old beams. There's a fireplace at one end and a little alcove opposite, in which I shall have them place a tub of some sort, no matter if hot water is tuppence a bucket. The windows—there are two of them—have little diamond panes and open upon a peaceful, sloping countryside. The Firth of Forth lies on the other side of the house.

As I lean on the window-ledge, I eagerly inhale the soft air, clear and invigorating, fresh with the scent of gorse and heather off the highlands. Such luck! I am impatient to get on.

Mr. Ferguson, the innkeeper, has assured me he can find just what I want—at least I think he said so. Fortunately he has had guests from south of the Tweed, and I am confident I made myself understood,

[2]

although I cannot state positively that his answer confirmed it. I had not thought of this.

He is out now making arrangements. He will probably succeed, as he has a very shrewd eye and my remaining for two or three months is in the bargain. I can hardly wait for his return.

Just beneath my window is a sweet bit of garden which runs on toward a square, white house. A most comely girl has been raking and pruning in it for the past twenty minutes. There is something about her appearance that attracts my attention—probably because she is the first Scottish lassie I have closely observed.

She has strong, beautifully rounded arms and laughing brown eyes that take a glint of bright sunshine in them as, chancing to look up, she perceives me at the window. I believe, too, she is smiling, although of that I'm not quite sure, as I pretend to be gazing at the hills. Undoubtedly she is the daughter of the innkeeper.

She is fully as tall as Angelica but not quite so slender, and her step is more smooth and springy. Her cheek is dimpled and has rich natural color, while I have observed that Angelica is usually rather pale until she comes from the locker-house.

Really, I do not know why I make such comparison . . .

Ah—that will be Ferguson's knock now.

"Losh, man! 'Tis the braw luck ye hae," he greets me. At least it sounds like that. From his smiling face I judge his news is encouraging.

"You have arranged it?" I ask eagerly.

"I'm tellin' ye. Sssh!" he adds in a confidential whisper. " 'Tis th' Macgrigurr himsel'!" and he steps back, apparently to enjoy my astounded delight; but I expect my face is as blank as my mind.

"He's th' greatest man in th' three counties. Recht noo he'd be champion o' them a', only Sandy's a wee bit odd at times an' nae owerfond o' th' croods. An' ae time at Musselburra—but I'll be tellin' ye that ower a pint o' ale o' evenin's. Ye're stayin' on th' noo, for so we agreed man tae man. Your room'll be sax shillin's th' week, wi' clean linen for th' bed everra third day; tuppence for candles; eightpence for soap an' towels, saxpence for breakfast, an' a shillin'——"

"Yes, yes," I interrupt; "but about this—ah—Sandy?"

"He'll dae it, I hae been tellin' ye, although 'tis tae favor me he consented. Ye'll gie him twa pund th' week."

"Where will I find him? Can I go to him now?"

"He's waitin' for ye. Ye just gae up tae th' end o' the road an' turn east. Cast your ee aboot for a lum—Garebrig lum—an' hauld straight for that till ye come tae Gannie Clark's wynd. Tak a turn up

[4]

there an' ye'll see a wee white housie back frae the road. Just gang in."

Now how am I ever likely to find him from that? True the village is small. In time no doubt I might come to him, but I am impatient.

"I go up this road," I begin; "turn this way——"

"Nae, nae. I canna gie th' day tae ye, laddie. Come, I'll show ye."

After a few minutes' walk to the right—I was sure he had told me just the opposite direction—the inn-keeper stops and indicates a small cottage at the end of a lane; it is on a little hilltop and set well apart from its neighbors. I thank him. In reply to his question, I assure him I can find my way back, and stride happily onward.

As I come near, I see there is a smaller building in the yard of the cottage. Over its door is a sign which, confirming all my hopes, fills me with joy.

I read:

Sandy Macgregor
Club Maker

And now you have my secret. It was my brilliant thought to learn this elusive art of golf right in its native heather.

With a feeling of trepidation, I approach the open door. I am now about to meet the man who will decide my destiny. I pause and take mental resolution that I will place myself entirely in this man's hands; I will heed the least thing he tells me and never neglect to do it!

I knock—perhaps a little timidly, for already I sense victory in my grasp and I wish to assume that bearing of modesty that rests so becomingly on all our best players.

There is no answer, although I seem to hear the light sound of some movement.

I knock again—louder.

"Weel," rumbles a deep voice from within, "nae doot ye can see th' door's open."

I step more into view and enter the single room.

My nostrils are greeted by an intriguing scent of varnish and turpentine and oil.

My eyes, prepared to meet some kindly smiling face, see first a confused tangle of fishing rods, landing nets and golf clubs suspended from the wall or set upright on a broad shelf which holds an even more complicated litter of the same objects together with paint pots, brushes, hand tools, a bundle of unworked shafts, unmounted heads and irons, reels, flybooks and a scattered medley of flies.

At a glance I perceive it is the work of tying a fly which at the moment engages the man whose broad back is toward me. I observe the huge shoulders, the gray hair of a massive head covered by a

[6]

battered soft hat and bent forward to his task, and the strong, bronzed hands which seem too large for such a delicate operation.

Of course, the impossibility of interrupting this work, once started, has prevented him from rising to greet me.

I wait—while his thick fingers set a bit of bright feather against the shank of a hook, wind the thread around it with extraordinary deftness, touch it with shellac and, putting the fly aside—reach out to take up another.

"I believe this is Mr. Macgregor?" I venture,

"Tae my ain knowledge, there's nae man sae ca'ed in a' th' Elie," rumbles the giant.

"Ah—I beg pardon. But—Mr. Ferguson pointed out this place to me—and," with sudden inspiration, "the sign above the door?"

A silence endures while he holds an end of thread in his teeth, to commence another winding.

"Ma name's Macgrigurr—Sandy Macgrigurr."

"Oh—then I'm right after all."

"Ye're nae recht an' ye're nae wrang." Another interval. "Ye can ca' me Sandy. A' th' boys dae."

While I am pondering this, not exactly pleased at my classification, he turns leisurely around to face me.

A great head with wide-set, keen, twinkling gray eyes under the old brim; cheeks of deep bronze, wrinkled like a russet apple in winter, above a heavy beard of iron-gray; huge shoulders and deep, broad chest in flannel shirt and old coat; worn trousers over stalwart legs—this is Sandy Macgregor.

"Ye'll be Robert Hale. An' ye want tae learn th' game o' gowf."

The shrewd eyes measure and plumb me in one swift glance. Under their direct look, I feel not one whit bigger or better than I am. However, their bright twinkling gives me a little reassurance.

"Yes, Mr.—ah—Sandy, I should like to take lessons from you. What I want most of all is——"

"A' recht; then we'll commence."

"But first let me give you a week's advance. Mr. Ferguson told me——"

"It's nae necessary. If ye rin awa an' nae pay me, I'll get it frae him. He taks a farthin' frae everra shillin' ye are to gie me anyway."

"What!" I cry. "You say, Mr. Ferguson——"

"It's a canny man is this Bob Ferguson."

"No! I pay you what I agreed. I'll give him his commission in one lump."

"Verra weel, Robert," he returns placidly. "Noo we'll commence."

"Shall I take off my coat?" I ask, looking around for a suitable driver. For this first interview I had left my clubs at the Inn.

[8]

He makes no move to leave his chair.

"What was th' first large toun ye come tae in Scotlun'?"

"Edinburgh," I answer promptly.

"Hey?"

"Edinburg."

"Na! Na! Ed'nbur-ra! Say it."

"Edinboro."

"Nae!"

"Edinburo."

"Nae! Ed'nbur-ra!"

"Edinbura."

"Ed'nbur-r-a; Bur-r-a!"

"Buro."

"Bur-r-a!"

"Bura."

"Bur-r-r-a!"

"Burra!"

He reaches out his great hands, and with one grasps my forehead and with the other holds my chin.

"Say it again th' noo, Robert. Ye're yappin' wi' yer head like a dug. Can ye no say Ed'nbur-ra an' stand still, man?"

"Edin-bur-ra!"

He withdraws his hands.

"Ance mair, laddie."

"Edin-bur-ra," I repeat obediently; and, feeling a little natural resentment at such familiarity, add: "But I want to learn golf, not the language."

"Ye hae just haed th' maist important lesson in a' gowf—tae keep yer head frae waggin' whatever ye're aboot. That's a' fer th' day, Robert," and he turns to his bench. "Ye can come th' same time th' morrow—an' if I'm nae at hame, it'll mean I've gaen feshin', an' the next day'll dae as weel."

II

I HAVE frequently observed at home that in our haste to play creditable golf, an excellent principle we may receive from one instructor is either contradicted or replaced by advice from too many other teachers and insistent friends, so that we often forget its importance.

Having this fact in mind and being assured that the word of Sandy Macgregor is law, I am determined to preserve careful record of every separate point he gives me and religiously practice one and all until they become second nature with me. In that way, I am sure to achieve success.

I, therefore, make my first entry:

Keep the head motionless.

And, after a most excellent supper, I spend considerable time in my room, practicing this precept in as many ways as I can devise without taking a club in my hand. While watching my head in a mirror, I even repeat vehemently that word—Edinbur-ra—which so fills the mouth with rolling r's.

During this latter part, I hear light bursts of

laughter from the garden below my open windows;
no doubt the innkeeper's daughter with friends,
amused by something they do not understand. But I
will not be distracted. This is a serious work I have
set myself to do each evening following the lesson of
the day, and I will allow nothing to divert my mind
from concentrating upon it.

Strange what bright, intelligent eyes that girl has.
Altogether, brown eyes seem to possess a warmth and
depth peculiarly their own, suggesting capacity for
feeling and less calculation where emotion is involved.
. . . Angelica's are blue. . . .

I am so elated with my success in securing such a
famous Scottish instructor that I wonder if I should
not send a cable to Angelica preparing her for my
worthiness of consideration.

In thinking about the matter, I become drowsy.
This old, four posted bed is so comfortable; the air
is cool, soft and fragrant; the little village, early to
retire, so quiet and peaceful. . . . That laughter was
like the rippling of a joyous brook. . . . I am surprised the innkeeper should have such a lovely
daughter. . . . How graceful and strong she appeared, with her erect figure, bare rounded arms and
in the short skirt that showed her free, easy
stride. . . .

*   *   *

Out of the Rough

I seem hardly to have slept at all, when I am awakened by a flickering light in my eyes and the sound of a heavy step on the uncarpeted floor of my room.

It is Bob Ferguson. His broad face is smiling; his shrewd eyes have a merry twinkle. He appears amused—— I wonder why.

"Come—oot wi' ye. Sandy's below an' there's a grand breakfast cookin'."

"What's the matter—it isn't even daylight!"

"What odds is that? Sandy is here to gie ye yer second gowf lesson. Dae ye ken the chief toun in a' Scotlun'?"

"Edinbur-ra," I answer mechanically, struggling into my clothes, but with my neck stiff.

"Guid fer ye, lad," and he gives me a strong clap on the shoulder. "We'll mak a gowfer of ye yet, an' I hae nae doot a' the village wull hae a han' in't," and Bob Ferguson roars with laughter.

"Shall I take my clubs?"

"Ye'll leave a' that tae Sandy. Listen, laddie," he adds, lowering his hearty voice. "He maun taen a likin' to ye, or he wudna gie ye th' rare treat he has fer ye this mornin'. Noo ye mind whatever th' auld boy says an' ask no questions. Dae everything, mind, just as he tells ye an' ye'll hae something nae man yet got oot o' Sandy Macgrigurr."

I find him sitting in the flickering candle light,

with a steaming cup of tea at his elbow and a plate
of sizzling ham and eggs just placed before him,
which so engrosses his attention he has only a nod
and a growl for my friendly greeting. I make haste
with my own breakfast, surprised by my appetite at
such an unearthly hour.

Sandy is wearing his old battered hat even at
table. It is curiously decorated with a great number
of bright colored flies with the snells interwound or
hanging over the brim. Apparently we are going
some distance from the Inn, for Ferguson is putting
sandwiches and several bottles of ale into a covered
basket having a little square hole in the top. It has
a broad webbing belt fastened to one side, and this
Bob slings over my shoulder, as I hurriedly finish a
second cup and am ready.

Sandy has lit his pipe and now takes from a corner two slender brown cases and—a landing net.

My second golfing lesson! Surely this looks more
like fishing tackle. However, in time I remember Ferguson's advice, catch his wink and broad grin and
silently follow Sandy into the gloom that precedes
dawn.

In a few minutes we are out of the village and
leave the winding road for a straighter way across
fields drenched with dew. Sandy stalks silently ahead
of me at a pace that soon makes me forget the rather
penetrating coolness. He bulks a huge figure in the

gloaming. Over his shoulder, the reek of his pipe wafts back to me.

We pass a little farm cottage. There is a light in the window; from the chimney, smoke curls straight upward—we shall have a clear day. In the east, the stars are paling and a glow is spreading; birds are commencing to cheep in the gorse thickets; the air is sweet and strong.

We climb a short slope and turn to go downward. Slowly the mists rise from bottom and hollow and reluctantly bare the face of the water. Soon behind us, against the growing light, the Firth of Forth lies gleaming like a broad strip of burnished silver.

Sandy walks less swiftly now; we are crossing a bit of lowland, and he is taking care with his steps. But my thoughts are not on him. In my nostrils is the scent of the Scottish heather we are treading. I feel the call of coming day, and my courage and ambition rise to meet it. I shall be victorious in my endeavor; already I picture my success—— My spirit soars—my eyes, uplifted, are upon the golden shafts Phoebus is hurling into the vaulted blue—and then suddenly I fall to earth.

I am waist deep in a bog-hole. The basket strikes the soft ground with a clatter of bottles; over his shoulder, Sandy throws me a reproachful glance.

I scramble out and follow his steps, with my lesson understood. One cannot reach the goal by thought

[15]

alone and in single flight, but must overcome, one by one, the obstacles that lie between. . . .

The sun is peering over the low horizon as we approach a broad, placid stream.

Sandy knocks out his pipe. He strips the case from the slender tips, rubs the ferrules against his nose, and joints the rod. From a pocket he takes a reel and sets it between the bands low on the butt; it screams shrilly as he swiftly draws the line through the guides.

A six-foot, dampened leader is unwound from his hat and tied on. He glances at the sky, then selects a small fly of crimson and white which he attaches to the drop; another, of brown, is fastened to the lowest loop. Giving me the second rod, in its case, he motions me backward to his left and steps farther on the bank. The landing net is hooked to his belt.

Out in the dark, smoothly flowing stream, nearer the opposite shore, there is a swirl where a fish has risen lazily in the cool water but has not broken the surface. Sandy fixes it with his eye. I am all haste and eagerness; but he coolly grasps the line with his left hand, close to the reel, and draws out an arm's length. He tosses the flies before him; a backward switch of the rod runs out the slack and carries the line behind. As it straightens, his arm moves slowly forward and a flick of the wrist casts the flies above the surface.

[16]

Out of the Rough

Before they can touch, he draws out more line; the slow backward sweep takes it up; again the forward motion and flick; the line loops and curves and the flies alight softly on the water just where I had marked the rise.

But simultaneously, six feet downstream comes another lazy swirling. The trout is working that way.

Sandy raises his arm until the line is straighter, gives a quick flip and slow backward movement. The flies leave the water without dragging the leader, and float behind him, then with the cast, settle as light as thistledown just below the last rise.

A sudden swirl, a faint splash. Sandy quickly lifts his wrist. The line instantly tautens with a bending of the slender tip, then cleaves the dark water with the long rush upstream; the reel sings merrily.

Sandy checks slightly; the rod bends half double and he gives more line slowly with his left hand. The rush is stopped and he takes in swiftly lest the tip should straighten, then feeds again as the green silk thread cuts back the other way. With difficulty I restrain myself from rushing to his side.

Abruptly the tip bends violently, straight downward. Slowly the line slips through Sandy's fingers. He checks it and the tip bends again and again. Now he begins to draw in—an inch, a foot, a yard. The thumb of his right hand holds the gain.

There is a loud splash on the surface; another

short run patiently recovered. Further splashing, more and more feebly. The fish is floating on its side and is being drawn steadily toward the shore.

Sandy unhooks the net, steps close to the water and, holding the bent rod high, with a quick scoop lifts a splendid trout safely to the bank. I hurry forward to look. It is brown, flecked with black and crimson spots.

Sandy steps back and leisurely fills his pipe. Then he cuts a light fork from a bush, thrusts one branch through the gills and gives me the trout to carry. It weighs about a pound.

By the time the sun is well up, he has ten of such beauties. I had not observed the passing of time.

We have worked downstream until we have come to a narrow, deep brook that runs into the river with a sharp bend. Just below the junction is a broad pool. The opposite bank is lined with bushes; our shore is clear.

"Noo, Robert,"—the first words from Sandy's lips that day—"Yester ye haed yer lesson tae keep yer head still. A' mornin' I hae been giein' ye th' second which, nae doot, ye hae been maist carefu' tae observe."

"I don't understand," I begin in great surprise.

"It's the free motion of yer arm awa frae th' body, an' a flick o' th' wrist at the proper moment. Tane an' tither are maist important, and besides baith, ye

[18]

hae seen ae thing mair. Fer everra fesh, ye hae rin up like a dug crazy wi' excitement, while I hae na turned a hair. Ye maun keep cool, Robert, if ye would learn th' game o' gowf."

While he talks, he is taking his rod apart and setting up the other which I see at once is neither so fine nor so slender.

"I'll gie ye a Jock Scott here—'tis th' weightiest fly I hae by me. Noo, joomp over to that bit of high bank. Ye wull hae naithing but th' burn behind an' th' river in yer face. There are no fesh here fer ye tae scare an' ye can practice what I hae showed ye."

I did not wish to confess it, but the fact is, in my interest in the fishing, I had taken little notice of the fine points of Sandy's casting except to admire the ease and dexterity with which he sent the flies an enormous distance to any place he desired. It had never before occurred to me that there was any similarity between fly-casting and the golf stroke.

Rather doubtfully, I take the rod from his hands, observe a sly twinkle in his shrewd gray eyes, which does not add to my reassurance, and, leaping the brook, climb to the little flat of level bank.

As he has said, before me is the broad face of the pool and ten feet behind me the steep bank down to the brook, in which my fly is hardly like to catch.

Meanwhile Sandy empties the basket of our lunch and puts in his trout covered with wet grass. Filling his pipe, he seats himself comfortably on the bank and, with a bottle of ale in one hand, is ready to proceed with my lesson.

"Staund square on yer twa feet; ye canna throw a fly or hit a gowf ba' on yer tiptaes. Keep yer head still an' do th' work wi' yer arm an' yer wrist. Noo!"

Although I have just seen the simple operation hundreds of times, on my first attempt the tip of the rod touches the ground behind me and when I endeavor to make the forward throw, the fly strikes me in the head with a stinging slap, catches my cap and whirls it into the water.

I recover it and extricate the hook in considerable chagrin. Sandy says nothing; but it seems to me the bottle gurgles expressively.

I keep at it and, by diligent effort, finally acquire sufficient skill to launch the fly a rod's length or more ahead of me.

"A wee bit mair time on yer backswing," cautions Sandy. "Start slow when the line is straight behind. Dinna sway yer body, noo, Robert. Gie it a flip o' yer wrist when yer arm gangs oot an' follow through wi' it. That's mair like it. Noo—slow an' even on th' back; slow on th' start—flick it—follow it oot. Noo, back ance mair—slow. Get yer timin' frae th' taut line. Keep yer body still, lad. Use yer arm free— that an' th' rhythum an' th' timin' mak th' gowf swing."

Watching the line carefully, I soon begin to get

[20]

the hang of it, wondering at the ease and simplicity with which the lesser effort brings better result.

When the arm comes freely forward at the proper speed and the wrist flicks at just the right moment, further and further sails the fly. I am delighted. Although my whole arm commences to ache from the unaccustomed exercise, I am determined to master the movement until I am certain I shall retain it. For Sandy has said that it resembles the golf swing.

Sandy has fallen silent for a little, and I hear the popping of another cork.

"Steady, noo, Robert. Dinna be hurried. Ye'll never mak a gowfer if ye canna keep cool. Noo—draw oot a little mair slack—hauld it fer yer oot swing. Tak it up slow—noo, back—forrard—flick it——"

I watch the fly float swiftly through the air a full six feet further than I have yet cast. With the rod horizontal, proudly I wait for it to touch the water, to draw it back and make another equally as far.

It settles lightly—there comes a tremendous swirling, the flash of something dark and a resounding flop. In my surprise, I must have jerked my hand involuntarily, for a strong pull yanks viciously at the slender rod; the reel fairly screams as the swiftly running line cuts across the pool.

A wild roar from Sandy nearly proves my undoing.

"Gie her th' butt! Gie her th' butt! Keep yer finger free o' th' line—hauld yer rod up, man! Nae let that tip gae slack or I'll brain ye wi' th' bottle I hae in ma han—— Noo! Tak her in slow—wi' yer left han'—*wi' yer left han'!* Man, y're akwart! Steady—dinna jerk it. When she rins tither way, let it oot through yer fingers—slow!—Keep th' butt doun an' th' tip up, I tell ye! If ye lose that fesh, I'll strangle ye wi' ma ain twa hands—noo! She's comin' toward ye! In wi' yer left—steady—— *Keep—that—butt —down!* Easy noo—— Let her rin! Noo she turns. Dammit—if I cud anely get tae ye an' tak that rod. Gawd A'mighty, man—keep th' tip in the air!"

As the fish turns again and rushes upstream, I have a glimpse of Sandy from the corner of my eye. He has dashed his hat to the ground; his long gray hair is waving wildly and, with a bottle in one hand, he is dancing up and down like a maniac.

"Hauld tae it, lad!" he roars. "Dinna leuk at me —keep yer ee on th' *fesh!*—— She's weakenin'—keep th' strain on her—if ye gie her an inch o' slack, as ma name's Macgrigurr, I'll hae th' life o' ye! Noo she's comin' up—— Hauld her steady!"

There follows a great splashing and flopping. With what strength I have I try to follow Sandy's bidding, although my wrist and arm ache so painfully I fear I cannot hold the rod much longer.

"Look oot! Let her hae it slow—she winna rin far —*quick!* Yer tip! Up wi' it! She's risin' again—noo

[22]

—draw her in—slow—an' steady—she's fair spent
—— Watch oot, man! She'll try it ance mair, an'
let her hae a little. Be firm an' gentle wi' her. She's
up again an' sidin'—draw her in—steady, I tell ye!
Pint yer rod tae me—bring her in th' burn here—
keep her comin'—keep her comin'. My Gawd—what
a fesh!"

Sandy steps forward into the water where the
brook joins the river. With the net in one hand, he
still grasps the bottle with the other.

The fish is wallowing on the surface. At his direction, I pull the line in slowly, endeavoring to keep the
rod up with my quivering right hand.

Nearer and nearer, it approaches him. But now
I have no longer the strength to maintain the strain
and, grasping the butt with both hands, I commence
to walk slowly backward, fearing each moment the
fish will make another rush and break away from the
tight line.

"Keep tae it, Robert lad—ower this way—I canna
soom fer her—steady noo—ae foot mair——"

But what happens then, I cannot say.

Suddenly the ground gives away beneath my feet.
I feel myself falling backward a great distance.
There is a savage yell from Sandy, and the water of
the brook closes over my head.

When I finally succeed in getting my feet under
me and start to scramble out of the brook, I find that

I still clutch the rod in both hands. It is for that reason, I expect, I was like to drown, for it was with great difficulty I had been able to get my head above water.

To my consternation, there is no longer any strain on the rod. The line hangs loose and the fly comes flopping down to me as I pull it in. The fish must have torn away as I fell. It was probably an unusually large one, to judge from Sandy's excitement. I can not see him at the moment and I hear not a sound. In some trepidation, I crawl up the bank.

Sandy is standing on the opposite side of the brook, gazing at the ground. At his feet lies one of his own trout. Beside it is another, quivering and gasping; it is fully twice as long.

I spring across and join him; but he neither looks at me nor says a single word.

With my shoes sloshing and the water streaming from my clothes, I daresay I make an amusing appearance, but Sandy does not laugh; I do not once catch his eye turned in my direction. To my surprise, he also is wet.

In silence we eat our sandwiches and share the two remaining bottles of ale. Without a word he fills his pipe, replaces the rods in their cases, picks up the basket of fish and leads the long way home.

When we enter the lane close by his cottage, he

stops, and taking the big trout from the basket which it nearly fills, gives it to me.

"Robert, man," he says slowly; "I fair believe ye'll mak th' grandest gowfer in a' th' warld."

"Do you really, Sandy?" I cry, elated. "I thought, myself, I was getting that arm and wrist motion much better toward the end."

"It's nae that I mean, Robert," he answers, and I wonder at the sadness of his tone. "Skill hae muckle tae dae wi' gowf—I'll nae gainsay that. But, laddie, if ye ever drive yer ba' aff the line amang the whins, ye'll find it a' teed up fer ye nice an' fine. Ye're possessed, Robert, o' the luck o' th' deil himsel'. Noo —I've whupped that same bit o' water, up an' doun, forrard an' back, fer full thirty year—an' never hae I seen a fesh like that."

III

So my second entry is:

> A firm balance with the weight on the heels:
> Use the arms free from the body, with a flick
> of the wrist at the right time.

For a while I practice this—before the mirror, with various postures; but my wrist is lame and altogether I am exceedingly tired. I seek my comfortable bed early. . .

I am dreaming of Angelica. She is standing in the heather and is singing. I seem even to hear the song:

> *"A rosebud by my early walk, adown a corn-
> enclosèd bawk,*
> *Sae gently bent its thorny stalk, all on a dewy
> morning."*

I expect the curious fact that Angelica is using Scottish words arouses my mind to conjecture, for slowly I awaken. Yet, strangely, in place of losing the song, I fancy that I hear it more clearly:

OUT OF THE ROUGH

*"Ere twice the shades o' dawn are fled, in a' its
crimson glory spread,
And drooping rich the dewy head, it scents the
early morning."*

There follows an interval of silence, while I
struggle with this peculiar phenomenon.

Then something light and damp strikes my cheek
with a breath of sweet fragrance. I open my eyes
and discover beside me on the pillow a full blown
rose moist with dew.

My thoughts gather quickly. I crawl from the bed
and, possessed of a suitable sense of modesty, cau-
tiously raise my head to the window-ledge.

Down there in the garden is the innkeeper's
daughter. Her back is toward me as she walks slowly
away between the rose bushes. Her head is bare and
I observe that her hair is a rich, glossy brown with
a glint of bright gold where the sun strikes it. There
are little curls, too, at the firm, white neck.

She glances upward over her shoulder at the sky.
I catch a sparkling flash in one brown eye and duck
hastily from sight. As I crawl backward further into
the room, I hear a chuckle of laughter.

*"So thou, sweet rosebud, young and gay, shall
beauteous blaze upon the day,
And bless the parent's evening ray that
watched thy early morning."*

[27]

Now that I know who it is, I am surprised at the excellence and culture of her singing voice. There is also a vague emotional timbre in the gay tones, like tears behind laughter, which gives me an unaccountable prickling in my throat. How can such a poor girl of her lowly station, the daughter of an ordinary hotelman, be so peculiarly charming. Why, even without her singing, she is—er. . . .

For some reason I make haste with my toilet. Ferguson has found me a broad tin tub. There is a bucket of hot water outside the door, and another, very cold, with which to finish.

As I descend to the common room of the Inn, where one's meals are served and which has at one end kegs of beer and ale on tap, I am astonished at the unusual sight of a group of several people. And apparently they are waiting for me. At my entrance they abruptly cease a very lively talking, and Ferguson calls:

"Ah—noo ye are here, mister Robert, we'll prove I am nae th' leear these guid folk verily believe," and he starts to leave the room.

With my thoughts on other things than the affair of yesterday, I am at a loss to understand; and while I wait in a little uncertainty, a fine looking man steps toward me—a gentleman, as I see at first glance. He is tall and of powerful build, yet I am more attracted by the intelligence of his features and the kindliness of his keen eyes.

"Ye are Mr. Hale," he greets me, with a cordiality and a courtesy of manner I would hardly have expected from the homely roughness of his dress. "I am John McPherson."

" 'Tis the minister of th' Elie," calls Ferguson over his shoulder; "an' a recht fine man for a' that."

He laughs as we shake hands. I like him instantly, and find something vaguely familiar in his expression although I cannot recall that I have ever seen him before.

"This is Angus Macbirnie," explains Mr. McPherson, indicating a broad shouldered, thick-set man, bareheaded and wearing a long leathern apron. His rolled up sleeves display huge, brawny arms; the open shirt—above the high apron—shows his muscular chest and thick, corded neck. His great hands are sooted. He seems to have stepped straight from his smithy.

"I'se na say Bob Ferguson's tellin' a lee," remarks the giant, in a deep, strong voice; " 'specially sin he taen his oath tae't. But I'm powerful keen tae hae a keek at yon fesh."

"Ay, he swore ye hae cleekit ae awfu' grand trout," pipes a thin, wiry little man beside him, who has eyes as sharp as a ferret's.

[29]

"And this is Tammie McLean," introduces Mr. McPherson in his pleasant, smiling way. "He is the postman of our village."

"Losh, man! I 'maist forgot it," ejaculates Tammas, digging in his pockets. He takes out several letters and, after looking at each one carefully, hands them all to me. "Thought there was anither, master Hale—a card or sic—like," and he fumbles further without result.

"If it's a card, Tammie's nae haed time yet tae read it," chuckles a third man sarcastically, a very tall, spare fellow, with a red nose and somewhat watery eyes.

"Dinna fash yersel' aboot that, Jamie Broun," retorts the wee postman sharply. "If ye wud min' your ain business of clerkin' as weel as Tammie does his, th' neebors wudna hae naithing to tulzie aboot."

Over Mr. McPherson's shoulder, I perceive the innkeeper's daughter quietly enter the long room and approach us with an expression of merry curiosity. Without thinking, I bow to her as I had to the men, and she instantly responds with a nod and a smile.

In the dull, heavily beamed room with its wood panelling and its various scents and odors, she is like a breath of the sweet morning. Of course, without studying her closely, I am nevertheless impressed by her fresh beauty, for, near-by she is lovelier than ever. Nor do I perceive in her face any resemblance to Bob Ferguson's rather heavy features; while her manner is neither shy nor forward. Altogether she appears a very attractive young lady, but, to be sure, this is my first sight of a Scottish country lassie and for all I know she may not be an unusual type.

In that first glance, she observes the rose in my lapel and rich crimson becomingly flushes her cheeks. After that, she does not look directly at me.

"Bob tells us you were out fishing," remarks Mr. McPherson, and I observe that his eyes are keenly amused. "We were discussing the merit of his story _____"

"An' noo ye can a' judge for yersel's," interrupts Ferguson from the doorway, and he comes toward us bearing a great platter covered with wet moss on which is my trout.

"Ma Gawd, man!" ejaculates the blacksmith, while the others push forward. "Ye hae na gien it strong eneugh, Bobbie."

"Fegs! It's ae buirdly fesh," adds the clerk. "What'll she weigh, man?"

"Three pund, twa ounce as she lays," answers Ferguson proudly.

"What water did ye tak her in?" asks the postman, slyly.

"I do not know," I reply. "Sandy did not tell me the name of the river, and I'm a stranger here you know."

"Good for you, Mr. Hale," and Mr. McPherson laughs heartily. "That's the first rule among fishermen—'dinna gie awa a guid water'!"

"An' what hae ye coost for't?" persists Tammie, poking the fish with his finger.

"What fly did you take it with?" interprets the minister.

"Oh—a Jock Scott," I answer with the casual manner of one altogether familiar with the art.

"Hum!" comments the postman reflectively and eying me with a peculiar expression. "A recht powerfu' fallow is this same Jock Scott. Wull ye hae a leuk at the clout he hae gien agee th' head o' the puir fesh!"

Surprised, I bend closer. Surely enough—on the side of the big trout's head shows clearly a mark as if it had been struck.

Suddenly I recall the appearance of Sandy Macgregor as I had seen him just before I so abruptly left the scene—knee deep in the water, the net in one hand, ready for the scoop, his precious bottle of ale brandished in the other. When next I saw him he was dripping wet to the shoulders.

I have not thought of it since or questioned his manner of landing the fish; but now I conjecture what might have happened with Sandy while I was floundering out of sight in the brook. Picturing the

[32]

Three pund, twa ounce as she lays!

sight the two of us must have presented, I burst into
a roar of laughter.

The men of the village gaze at me soberly and in
no little amazement.

"Here, Bob," I say, to save myself explanations;
"in my country, when a man makes a hole in one or
gets a big fish like that, it is customary to set 'em
up. Ask the gentlemen what they will have."

With almost suspicious promptness, the three villagers repair to the tap with Ferguson. Perhaps the
custom is known elsewhere.

"Guid health to ye, mister," calls the mighty
blacksmith heartily, raising his pint.

"An' may ye mak anither sic braw swipe wi' yer
gowf," adds the little postman with a sly wink.

"I expect you are fair brust with your story, Mr.
Hale," says Mr. McPherson, "but you'll not let on
about Sandy. 'Tis well, lad; 'tis well. Never give a
comrade away——"

"Or he may do the same with you," I rejoin.

"Never Sandy. He's 'mair sparin' wi' his words
than auld Davie Hunter wi' his saxpence,' as the saying hereabout goes. Still I would give much to hear
it," and he turns again to admire the trout.

"Bob," I say to the innkeeper who has come back
to us. "How many will this fish serve?"

"Stuff't wi' crumbs, parsley, capers, melted butter,

a pinch o' pepper an' salt, an' bak't in butter," answers the canny Ferguson, "four or five guid men."

"Very well then, Bob; if Mr. McPherson will join us tonight at dinner——?"

"With great pleasure," answers the minister, busy estimating the length of my trout.

"With you, Bob, and Sandy there will be four, and"——I do not know what inspires me, except, perhaps, the democratic atmosphere of the place and no doubt curiosity over what seemed to me a strange anomaly—"and if your daughter will honor us?" I suggest, bowing to the girl who stands a little apart, her eyes shining with interested amusement.

"My——?" begins Bob.

"Most assuredly," urges Mr. McPherson, still intent on his examination. "It will be a rare party if we can persuade Sandy to converse."

I turn back to Ferguson. He is smiling delightedly.

"Miss Jeanie wull be maist obliged, sin the minister says it's a' recht," he assures me; and I bow again in acknowledgment of this introduction.

She really seems pleased. In fact, her joy is apparently so great that she is just bubbling over with merriment.

"And when Mrs. McPherson finds herself a little better," adds the minister, turning to me, "we shall expect you at the Manse. It's the big, white house just back of the Inn. . . ."

*　　*　　*

Before setting out for Sandy's cottage that afternoon, I take out all my clubs, wipe them carefully and make sure that the shafts are not becoming too dry. They seem like friends to me; for are they not to bring me victory?

For some time, too, I debate with myself as to the advisability of taking some of them along. It is all very well to get the fundamentals clearly in my mind before putting the theories into actual practice, and I pride myself that I have thoroughly absorbed the two main principles which Sandy has made plain to me in such simple and convincing manner.

In fact, when one has a club in his grasp, the mind is so intent upon swinging it in some sort of stroke, one is not in most receptive condition and the full significance of vital points is rarely obtained. I fully approve of Sandy's method of impressing upon me the necessity of keeping the head motionless and using the arms free of the body. I am certain I shall forget neither.

However, I feel it is high time to commence actual work on my strokes and I have no doubt that, on this third day, Sandy has such intention. But, remembering Ferguson's advice, reluctantly I put away my

[35]

driver, of which I am very proud—it cost me fifteen dollars—and start up the road empty handed.

Sandy is not in his shop.

I am speculating whether my luck of yesterday has induced him to try that particular water again when, stepping from the door, my attention is attracted by a regular thumping in the direction of another little shed at the rear of the cottage. No one is to be seen about the place, so I start to investigate.

As I approach, the sounds cease and Sandy himself comes out of the narrow door, holding in his hand what appear to be two stout sticks fastened end to end.

Without responding to my greeting, he seats himself a little wearily on an old saw-horse leaning against the shed. His hat and coat are off, and I observe that he is perspiring.

"Noo, Robert; ye wull staund here afore me while I explain something further."

In some wonderment, I draw nearer.

Sandy leisurely fills his pipe and puffs a few moments in obvious enjoyment.

"Full mony a beuk," he begins, "has been writ aboot the eentricacies o' the stroke of gowf, I ken verra weel. But, Robert, I wudna fill yer pow wi' a' that. Just a few essentials ye maun ken an' when ye understaund them tae ma ain satisfaction, ye'll nae hae deeficulty in hitting the ba'. Noo—ye wull tell me what ye hae learn't."

"Keep the head still; have the weight firmly on the feet; use the arms free of the body, with a flick of the wrists at the right moment."

"Verra weel said, Robert; an' ye mauna forget. Then we can gang on. Maist folk, when ye gie 'em a gowf club, swipe th' ba' as if they were swinging a scythe or chopping wood. That's a' wrang; for there's nae sic force or weight required. It's the tap of th' club head that sends the ba' awa, an' when ye understaund that, ye wull perceive a heavy, slodging blow wi' the shouthers and the body nae allows th' club head tae dae its business.

"Mind ye, Robert," he repeats very seriously, "it's the club head that drives the ba', an' nae your shouthers, nae your body."

Up to this moment in my brief acquaintance with Sandy Macgregor, I have found him the most taciturn man I have ever known. I recognize immediately that his present mood is rare. What occasioned his good feeling toward me, I do not know; but I listen with almost breathless attention, aware, as Bob Ferguson had promised, that I am receiving what probably no other man ever had from him.

"Noo, Robert; it is necessary ye hae clear in your mind just how th' club works, for ye maun always be thinking ye're hitting the ba' wi' the club an' nae wi' your body."

Sandy lays down his pipe and walks toward the shed.

"Come here, Robert; I'll show ye. This threshin'-tree wull gie ye the proper idea—but dinna be confused. It is nae the swipe o' my arms that I want ye to observe. Keep your ee on th' handle an' th' swingle. It's th' swingle that beats th' grain frae th' wheat, an' it's the gowf club that hits the ba' frae th' tee."

Sandy kicks a small pile of wheat together on the floor and, raising the flail, makes a half dozen slow strokes which produce a heavy thumping.

"Dae ye see, Robert, how th' swingle flies forrard tae its work when it's swung proper? Noo, when I throw th' handle too hard an' too soon there's naithing to't," and he proceeds to illustrate.

"That's what happens," he continues, resting on the long stick, "when ye throw your shouthers an' your body into th' gowf stroke. The club head drags behind an' draws across the ba' an' ye get your slice everra time. Ye maun treat yersel' like the handle o' this threshin'-tree, wi' your wrists the cord that haulds th' twa, an' get your club oot ahead just as ye hae seen me throw th' swingle. Here, tak it, Robert, an' fa' till't."

As Sandy illustrates and explains the matter, for

the first time in my whole golfing experience, the actual making of the stroke is clear to me in a flash of revelation. At that moment, I am quite certain I have never made one correct stroke since I first took up the game several years ago.

From the beginning, I had been cursed and haunted by a terrible slice with both wood and iron. Although I had tried numerous remedies I had never been able to conquer it; and I now see my failure was entirely due to my lack of comprehension of how the stroke is actually delivered. Now I understand how Angelica, with half my strength, would outdrive me until I was ashamed to play with her and she preferred other partners.

Just as Sandy has made clear, I had not been hitting with any snap to the club head, but had been lunging with all the strength of my shoulders and body, and for the first time the inevitable result is easily apparent to me.

These are golden words. This alone is worth the long trip across the ocean and my temporary absence from the field.

Hot with enthusiasm, I take the flail from his hands and set to work, keeping my eye on the flying end and trying all manner of awkward strokes until I discover just what combination of force and speed with the handle produces the loudest thump.

When finally I hit upon it, I go steadily on, un-

[39]

mindful of blistering hands and the pouring sweat, fearing I should lose the right idea. As fast as I need it, Sandy feeds more wheat to me and sweeps the chaff and grain aside; but I am not thinking of the work at all and only keeping constantly before me the visualization of the club head action from this illuminating point of view.

"Weel, Robert," remarks Sandy at length, and I observe how bright is his eye; "I'm satisfied ye hae th' idee th' noo—an' we hae nae mair wheat tae thresh."

IV

I SHALL not attempt this morning the entry of the third golfing principle which I have received from Sandy Macgregor. In spite of my methodical habits, I did not do so last evening and, while I am satisfied the matter lies very clearly in my mind, at the moment I do not recall it and am loath to make the effort to drag it forth and set it down in proper and lucid form. . . .

I must arrange with Ferguson for coffee in the morning. I do not approve of tea for breakfast; it has no stimulating effect upon me. . . .

Now, that is strange. From my bed, I perceive my cap on the floor, stretched carefully over my shoe-trees. And there are my shoes hanging from a hook in the wardrobe!

Really, I do not believe I came to my room last night in such confusion of mind as that transposition of my effects would seem to indicate. The Scottish ale is potent—no doubt of that; and there appeared no lack of it. But I am quite certain I was in every way sober.

Why—I even made a speech toward the end of

[41]

the dinner, and it must have been witty, for I distinctly recall how they all roared with laughter—even Sandy Macgregor. Of course I could not have succeeded so well if I had not been fully possessed of my faculties, since I am not adept in such matters.

But—my cap on the shoe-trees. I do not understand. I shall take a walk after my breakfast.

What jolly folk these simple people are. And what an excellent dinner Ferguson managed.

Promptly at six we were seated around the table in the alcove of the taproom, which Bob has set aside for me. On my right was Mr. McPherson, the village clergyman, then Sandy with Ferguson opposite him and Miss Jeanie—Bob's daughter—at my left.

There were roses and fern on the table. I expect Miss Jeanie arranged that; and with the white cloth and curious old pewter and silver, the whole had quite an air in the quaint, low-ceilinged room.

The girl was positively charming in simple, dainty white, with a red rose at her throat to match the rich, warm color of her cheeks. Her manner, too, was rather surprising to me. I recollect now how I decided to accept the situation and, even if she was the daughter of the innkeeper, to conduct myself toward her as to any lady of my acquaintance; and she responded in such fashion as to arouse my admiration. I have a suspicion, now I think about it, that I must have paid her more attention than I had anticipated—but she was so lovely and demure, and then it was altogether a merry little party.

She speaks in the dialect of the villagers, with a most engaging accent in a low, vibrant voice that so thrills one with its suggestion of melody. But it seems to me she also used quite correct grammar; although as to that, I may have confused her talk at times with the speech of Mr. McPherson who is a most cultured gentleman.

By Jove—I never before knew that one stuffed and baked trout. It was delicious. But then I came with a voracious appetite, due no doubt to my long work with Sandy's flail. I should rather dislike swinging it right now. I expect the movement would be apt to make my head ache.

They all appeared in excellent humor the moment we gathered. Mr. McPherson was carrying on a joke with Miss Jeanie, teasing her of some matter which sent the bright color flying into her cheeks. For all that, he has a very high—if not tender regard for her, which probably in some measure inspired my own attitude toward her. I do not understand it. She is not at all what I should imagine would be the daughter of a hotelman. However, I am finding many surprising features in this quiet little village of Elie.

"So you are teaching Mr. Hale to play golf, Sandy," remarked Mr. McPherson, with a merry twinkle in his eye, in the pause while the depleted fish was being replaced by some fine roast lamb.

Sandy emptied his pint and held the mug to the waitress.

"Oh—aye; an' as a gowfer, he'll mak a grand fesherman," returned the Scotsman, without a smile on his face.

"Yes, that was a most remarkable trout even for Fife waters," persisted the minister. "I observe Mr. Hale is very modest; he has not yet told me the story of the catch. Perhaps he has greater skill with the fly than we folk who stick to our old ways."

"Humph!" rumbled Sandy, deep in a fresh mug. Then he wiped the foam from his beard. "There's nae doot Robert is a rare 'un; an' as ye weel said, minister, he's of a verra retirin' deesposition. I mind when I was takin' in the trout, he was nae in secht ava."

Now that was my first intimation from him that he was aware how I had fallen into the brook.

"Oh, Sandy," spoke Miss Jeanie, with that suggestion of amusement in her tone, which they all have, even with sober face. "When I was comin' hame frae Grannie Robertson's this afternoon, I heard a maist awfu' thumpin' ahind your housie. Thought I, ye're uncommon late wi' your threshin'."

Sandy, who had raised his pint again, coughed so

[44]

that he could not at once reply, and I hastened to answer for him.

"I expect that was I, Miss Jeanie. He was explaining the proper action of the golf club and I was practicing it with the flail."

Whereupon Mr. McPherson and Bob burst into such laughter I thought them in a fair way to split their sides; while it seemed to me that she glanced at both reproachfully.

"At any rate, Robert," said Mr. McPherson with fine camaraderie, wiping his eyes; "you'll have to take me fishing some day when Sandy can spare you from these useful lessons. I'll be quite content to handle the net and creel, and will carry a club, too, in case you get another big one."

"I'll tell ye what, minister," spoke up Sandy abruptly. "I'm gaun tae mak a gowfer o' Bobbie yet. Gie us a fortnecht, an' if ye wud beat him, stroke for stroke, ye maun leave your brechame at hame."

At this, Miss Jeanie, laughing until the tears ran down her cheeks, explained to me that "brechame" is really a horse-collar and not at all the clerical neckwear which Mr. McPherson had on.

"Guid fer ye, laddie," roared Bob Ferguson. "Gien Sandy say that ye can warst th' minister, I'll hae a wad on ye mysel'."

And filling their mugs again, the three men drank

[45]

to my success as a golfer, to which toast I felt it encumbent to drain my own. That ale, cool, fresh and sparkling from the tap, was delicious; one consumed pint after pint without realizing it.

"How is that, Sandy; you think you can make a golfer of him in two weeks?" inquired Mr. McPherson who appeared to be enjoying himself hugely.

"There's ane or twa things aboot Robert which gie me grand confidence in 'im. He'll dae exactly as he's tauld an' he's verra persistent. Attour a' that, he's lucky—oh, man, he's lucky."

Now I do not know what induced Sandy to speak so encouragingly of me; especially since he has a reputation in Elie of speaking very little at all. Naturally I was exceedingly pleased by such praise from him.

"It is evident I shall have to look to my game," rejoined Mr. McPherson, with a very bright sparkle in his glance toward me, which suggested some thought besides that he expressed. "Frankly I believe there are few such practical instructors of golf in all Scotland as Sandy. His lessons are never wasted effort. You have already observed something of this, Robert."

Sandy growled an unintelligible comment into his mug.

"The art of golf is natural with our people," went on the minister. "My own theory is that proper playing is largely a matter of temperament—a self-control which permits the effects neither of nervousness nor of overeagerness. The stroke depends preëminently upon skill rather than strength, and it is only after the muscles have been thoroughly trained to their proper functions that strength can be applied at all. If done too early, the result is more often than not disastrous, and it is practically axiomatic that one's game will go from bad to worse, faults will develop that become more difficult to eradicate as they grow fixed in habit and altogether improvement is well nigh impossible. I think you follow me understandingly, Robert?"

Indeed, I was hanging on his words which so truly expressed my very own experience. However, I could not reconcile the merry twinkle in his keen eyes to the sober nature of this discussion. I observed, too, that both Miss Jeanie and Bob Ferguson were listening no less intently than I; and they appeared covertly amused at something which for the moment at least was quite beyond me. Even so soon I had learned that Scottish wit is not only keen and sometimes brusque, but as well often too subtle for a stranger to anticipate.

"Our boys," continued Mr. McPherson, "and our girls, as well," with a nod and a smile at Miss Jeanie, "learn the game young. The majority become expert; but very, very few have the ability to impart their skill to others. I, myself, could teach Latin, Greek and mathematics, for example, but I am sure I could not compare with Sandy as an instructor in golf."

" 'Tis weel said, minister," interjected Sandy, who had been confining the most of his attention to his plate and pint. "Maist anyone can be a dominie, but it taks a recht guid head tae teach gowf."

"Sandy has that rare gift *par excellence*," pursued the clergyman, sharing the laugh at his expense. "Now I am convinced that one of our outstanding national characteristics is modesty; and you can find no better example to prove my assertion than Sandy Macgregor here, who, to my mind, could have been open champion over and again."

Sandy turned a quick, suspicious glance upon Mr. McPherson; but the minister hastened to continue almost as if to forestall his interruption.

"Perhaps it was twenty years ago that some of us in Elie, who fully recognized his ability, prevailed upon Sandy to enter a match at Musselburgh."

He paused to drain his mug and, by singular coincidence, Sandy and Ferguson did the same. While the eyes of the three men were thus averted, to my surprise Miss Jeanie seized the opportunity to turn to me with a bright smile and one slender finger pressed to her lips.

[48]

"It followed close upon the championship which had been played at St. Andrews," resumed Mr. McPherson. "You see, Musselburgh was the home course of that year's winner with whom Sandy had his match. As I recollect, the stakes were twenty pounds. Am I right, Bob?"

"There was muckle mair than twenty pund to't," answered Sandy for him. "Twenty pund was the stake, put up by the men o' Musselbur-ra as a free gift to Bob Chambers. I hae nae doot it was what they fair owed him. I put anither twenty pund mysel' agee his ain. Then there was the train-fare tae get tae Musselbur-ra an' back; the bill at th' inn—nane of th' robbers wud tak me in th' necht—a broken club and my ba'. But let the minister tell his story. Eh, Bob, man; canna your kimmer fetch me a pint-stoup? There's naithing but froth in these sma' mugs, an' that nae gies a man a fair drink."

There was such a curious change in Sandy's manner that I commenced to catch a glimmer of the meaning of Miss Jeanie's warning. To indicate my quickening comprehension, I reached my hand below the table and, encountering her fingers, I pressed them slightly. As she did not withdraw them, they remained a short while in my clasp.

"I followed the match hole by hole," continued Mr. McPherson, turning a little from Sandy; "and I am certain I never witnessed a more interesting and exciting game. You must understand, Robert, that Chambers was at the very top of his form. He had just come from winning his second championship, while Sandy, due to that innate modesty to which I have referred, was altogether unknown in professional competitions.

"These facts contributed two important phases to the match. In the first place, Sandy's wonderful playing was bound to have its mental effect upon the champion who had everything to lose; while the men of Musselburgh eagerly seized the opportunity to back their favorite and, as they thought, win a lot of easy money from the Elie crowd who had come loaded with silver to place upon Sandy.

"You must keep in mind, too, that while all Scotsmen are keen and fair sportsmen, there are always bound to be some over-zealous partisans whose interest makes them forget at times the courtesy due a stranger and an opponent."

"Humph!" growled Sandy. "I ken, minister, ye hae a grand chareetableness toward a' sinfu' creatures, an' nae doot ye wud gie the deil himsel' a proper recommendation. For mysel', wha am nae sae righteous and dinna gang aft agley the trowth, I canna say ae guid word for any man o' Musselbur-ra."

"In Musselburgh are many workmen," continued

[50]

the minister, "miners and the like, rough fellows, close followers, and players too, of the national game, who have a great pride in one of their own. And it was with this partisan element Sandy was called upon to contend, in addition to playing the open champion."

"I declare tae ma Gawd," offered Sandy, as the minister paused, "it was awfu'! In ma time I hae seen mony a fecht, but never hae ma twa cen fall'n upon sic a secht of rowin' an' racin', roarin' an' ravin' as that crowd o' Musselbur-ra robbers gien us that day."

"Yes," continued Mr. McPherson, "it was a true test of a man as well as of a golfer, and we of Elie to this day are proud of the manner in which Sandy stood up to it. If it had not been for one bit of human frailty, to which we all are prone——"

"Minister!" interrupted Sandy, with much heat. "Man to man, hae ye never haed th' wish tae dae murder in your heart?"

"As I said," answered Mr. McPherson, biting his lip; "we all have our weaknesses, and I will confess I fully appreciated Sandy's feelings on that particular occasion. I might go further and state that I could not afterward explain the condition of my own knuckles when we finally made our way to the train.

"Well—the match was arranged, the date set and

[51]

the news of it gave a great stir not only in the two towns but also in Edinburgh and in fact pretty much throughout Scotland.

"Two days before the game, Sandy went to Musselburgh to become familiar with a course that was strange to him—testing the pace and character of the greens, locating the bunkers and other hazards and learning where best to play from the tee to help his second shots.

"I expect, Mr. Hale, you have scarcely anything in America that resembles some of our old Scottish links. There, I am told, you have hundreds of acres available for a club with one or two courses, with clear, broad fairways from tee to green. It is not often so with us and on practically all it takes a real good golfer to escape severe punishment before he is well home. Much of our early golf was played on commons and such odd bits and many of our links of today have developed from similar traditional ground.

"Musselburgh gives a fair example, dating from 1774. An old race track lies between a row of houses on Levenhall Road and the sea. Around and across this race course, with its barriers well in evidence, were laid out the nine historic holes demanding as sporty a bit of play as one could wish. Fences and railings, to say nothing of the sand of the shore, make wicked hazards.

"Who, that has swung a club in Scotland, or in England for that matter, does not know 'Mrs. Formans,' 'Pandy,' the 'Sea Hole,' the 'Gasworks'?

"With Sandy, of course went 'The Deacon,' his favorite caddie."

"An' a recht grand lad was th' auld Deacon," rumbled Sandy from deep in the new mug the girl had brought him, which I verily believe would hold almost two quarts.

"There's another thing that's probably new to you, Robert—our caddies," explained Mr. McPherson who was taking keen if leisurely enjoyment over his story. Observing the growing tenseness of Sandy's expression and the expectant interest evinced by Bob and Miss Jeanie, I suspected he was purposefully working upon the old golfer's feelings for some declaration of his own. As for myself, in such surroundings and rare company, with the evening before me, I did not care to miss a word, eager as I was for him to reach the climax in this experience of the great Macgregor.

"Our caddies, particularly of the old school—God preserve them to us—are not merely carriers of clubs for a shilling the round. They are counsellors, staunch supporters with the right word of encouragement or shrewd if scathing advice at the proper time. They know their man and his temperament, and they know his club, shot for shot and lie for lie.

"They may be good players themselves or they may not, although some of our most noted professionals were numbered among them; but to a man they know the game from every angle, and, losh! how they do take a match to heart!

"The Deacon was a true one of them—a weazened faced, wiry little old fellow, keen of eye as he was sharp of tongue; and he would rather have carried clubs all day long for Sandy than sit still in the sun and be paid for it. I do not believe he was ever the same after the match at Musselburgh."

Mr. McPherson paused for a fresh quaff of ale and a sidelong glance at Sandy; but Sandy sat with one great hand on his pint-stoup and his eyes on the table before him.

"The great day came at last," continued Mr. McPherson, "late in September—worst luck—with early dusk and a fog off the Firth.

"There was a noisy, confident little crowd that took train at Elie, sure of victory from the first and with their pockets bulging with all the money they could manage to scrape together. But we were a mere handful compared with the dense throng that lined both sides of the fairway and the railing and banked the first green as Sandy and Chambers went to the tee."

"Noo," suddenly spoke Bob Ferguson from a long silence, "just hauld a wee bit, minister, afore ye tee 'em off. It's a long, wet story ye're comin' tae, an' here's as fine a bowl of hot toddy as ever ye wet your lips wi'. An' lettin' it get cauld wull nae improve the taste o't."

At his signal, the girl placed before us a steaming bowl, redolent with a rare odor; and even Sandy roused himself with a muttered word of approval, while we all turned to do justice to this crowning example of Bob's art.

V

WE sat back while the girl removed the dishes and stripped the cloth from the heavy oaken table. We drew up again as she gave us fresh mugs with a cool, frothing pitcher and passed around the cigars I had brought from home, which Bob and Mr. McPherson accepted appreciatively, while Sandy drew forth his pipe.

I won't say we were any the worse for the quantity of that fine ale we must have drunk, or the tasty bit of hot toddy which followed it. Miss Jeanie had only sipped from her small pewter from time to time, and so far as I could observe, none of the men showed the least effect. For myself, I felt merely pleasantly exhilarated.

Surely I cannot ascribe to that, the rousing song with which Mr. McPherson favored us while the table was being cleared. It is called "The Carles of Dysart"—and Bob Ferguson roared out the chorus, in which Miss Jeanie and I joined, and Sandy banged out the time with his giant's mug, regardless how the little he had left in it splashed about.

Out of the Rough

"Hey, ca' through, ca' through,
For we hae mickle ado;
Hey, ca' through, ca' through,
For we hae mickle ado."

Really, it was one of the jolliest, merriest evenings I can well remember. The long, old, old room with its great ceiling beams dried and cracked and smoke grimed with the years; the boxes of geraniums in the low, small paned windows; the scent of the fresh ale and beer; the bare armed tapster, pausing ever and again in his busy occupation to catch some laughing phrase from our table set somewhat aloof at the farther end.

And lastly—best of all—these honest, hearty Scotch people gathered around me, from strong featured, weather beaten old Sandy Macgregor to sweetly smiling Miss Jeanie, intent upon making the stranger feel at home.

No—I will not say the toddy and the many pints of ale, I have no doubt were my unconscious portion, caused the warm glow of friendliness for this goodly company to spring up in my breast, or incited me to follow the minister with a ballad of my own. And, come to think of it, I was in uncommonly good voice, while it had been my veriest belief and the opinion of my friends that I could not sing at all.

The little interruption was a welcome respite in the rather hearty dinner canny Bob Ferguson had prepared for us, and seemed somehow to bring us all closer together in even greater sociability.

When the laughter and applause, which greeted my effort, had subsided—save for Miss Jeanie's continued chuckling—we all turned to Mr. McPherson, eager for him to go on with his story of Sandy's famous match at Musselburgh.

He recommenced his tale with an account of some local happening which, for the life of me, I cannot now recall; although I know it was extremely funny, for we all laughed uproariously. Then the girl brought me a cup of strong black coffee—which for some reason appeared to cause general amusement —and after drinking it, I listened more intently and with less inclination to laugh at passages which at the time struck me as absolutely ludicrous, although less so as I now think back upon them.

"I am exceptionally fond of playing," said Mr. McPherson, particularly addressing me, with his face wreathed in its broad, wholesome smile; "nevertheless, my greatest enjoyment is to witness an exhibition by two finished golfers who are so expert in their skill that they attempt and accomplish feats of play which reveal an altogether new phase of the game to those whose knowledge and ability are mediocre.

"For me, such a performance constitutes the best sort of lesson——"

[58]

"Wi' a' respect for th' reverence of your profession, minister," interrupted Sandy dryly; "ye are th' maist stubborn scholar o' gowf aye come under ma ain observation."

"He means, Robert, I have too many of my own ideas."

"Aye, that's ane o' your faults," agreed Sandy.

"At any rate," laughed Mr. McPherson good-naturedly, "I derive great benefit from watching a good match. I expect I observe the fine points in the execution of the shots, rather than following the flight of the ball. And I will say this; on the occasion of the Musselburgh match, others besides myself learned something altogether new in the way a particular stroke can be played, and it was our own Sandy who provided the surprise to as ardent a gallery as I have ever seen."

"Fegs! ye're recht there," growled Sandy, who appeared entirely recovered from his taciturnity. "They were nae lackin' in ardor."

"Some of the keenest students of the game in all Scotland were there, Sandy."

"Savin' th' crood frae th' Elie, I'll say they were ruffians tae a man."

"I, myself, saw a great many gentlemen from Edinburgh."

" 'Tis nae a gentleman wha'll nae staund up for th' rechts of a matter. Ye, minister, was a recht fine gentleman that day," added Sandy with a great laugh. "I parteecularly observed how guid ye mashed th' face of ae bauld robber tae help the cause o' the argument."

"Er——" continued Mr. McPherson hastily, with a quick glance at Miss Jeanie; "let me see—— I had brought you to the point where the match started, I believe, Robert."

"Aye," affirmed Bob Ferguson; "those tees hae been standin' a recht lang time."

"As the visiting player," continued the minister, "Sandy had the honor, and as he stepped to his ball, the perfect picture of coolness and confidence, the great crowd settled into some measure of quiet.

"His opening drive was beautiful. Such a clean hit with a free, easy swing that suggested rather than exposed the tremendous strength kept in proper reserve behind it. Straight as an arrow; correctly sent for direction—a bit to the right to clear the railing and open up the green for his approach.

"Robert, don't you envy the man who can judge his shot and play his ball just where he wants it to go?"

"Indeed," I answered almost reverently; "it is altogether an unopened book to me!"

"Chambers followed with one slightly longer; a cheer burst from the eager Musselburghers; the dense crowd swayed down the fairway, and the great match was on. Two perfect approaches; the customary two putts on the wide green, and a half in par four.

"From this beginning, the difference in golfing temperament between the two men was at once apparent. Without hurrying his shots, Sandy wasted not a second of time. A glance down the line; a look at his ball, and immediately the clean, crisp hit in the perfection of form.

"On the contrary, Chambers proved himself a careful, deliberate player, particularly around and on the green, studying every phase of his shot and putt before taking his stance and even then hanging over his stroke.

"One showed the master; the other, the painstaking plugger—and remember, Chambers had just won the open.

"Well, Sandy finished the first nine one up. Both men were playing as flawless golf as you could hope to see, but Sandy was the surer of himself, dared to take the longer chances and most certainly was wearing down the champion when the Musselburghers took a hand in the game.

"Right at the commencement of the second nine, one deliberately stepped on Sandy's long hit ball, grinding it into the turf and costing him a stroke and the hole; for the play was that close. And at 'Mrs. Forman's,' where the night shift from the mines joined the crowd, a man bumped into him as he was putting and cost him another.

"At the 'Sea Hole' for the second time, Sandy followed a fine drive with a perfect iron which to all appearances stopped on the green. Yet when we reached it, the ball was not to be seen, either on the green or immediately around it.

"In hunting for it, my attention was caught by the Deacon. He was the picture of dumb rage and despair. Half of Sandy's clubs were in the bag, the rest under his arm as, pulling at his long hair, he trotted back and forth like a trained setter quartering a field.

"Finally we observed a small group on the beach and, although they said nothing, it was evident from their manner they had found something. We didn't understand how Sandy's ball could possibly have gone that far, but we went over. And surely enough there it was—snugly in an old boot left by the receding tide.

"A roar of laughter went up from the Musselburgh miners and their friends as we bent over it. In our hearts, we knew well enough the ball had been kicked from the green and put in this impossible place—but how to prove it? Up to that point, the Elie men had ranged themselves close by Sandy and none of us had seen it done.

"Small wonder Sandy's anger boiled over. With a

heavy niblick he gave the boot such a clout that he lofted it clear over the low railing on to the green; but the ball still remained inside, and another shout of delight burst from the crowd."

"Aye and I would o' sunk th' danged thing for a half," growled Sandy; "only th' boot would na fit th' hole."

"Now, no human being could stand that forever, and Sandy finished the morning round one down when, but for the interference of the Musselburghers, he should have led by three.

"During the lunch hour, the town was in a turmoil of excitement, talking of nothing but the big match. And, fegs! they'd seen rare golf. Bob Chambers was their pride and they knew his play; but here was an outsider who, when undisturbed, had not once been over a most difficult par and with but one shot in the eighteen holes anywhere off the line—and that, after they had put his ball in a boot!

"Two friends took Sandy and the Deacon to a quiet place for lunch and a bit of rest; and that was all Sandy needed to bring him back to himself. In the afternoon, when he went again to the tee with Chambers, he was the picture of confidence, with a set to his jaw I knew right well. 'Now, you Musselburgh rooters,' said I to myself; 'you will see some golf.'

"It was Chambers' honor, from that disastrous

'Sea Hole,' and, taking plenty of time, his drive was a good one. Then the crowd turned to Sandy, curious to detect any signs of breaking.

"He teed up calmly, gave a long, hard look at the rows of densely packed faces, a glance down the line —and away went his ball, true as a rifle shot, yards beyond the champion.

"Chambers was worried and showed it by the way he lingered over every one of his shots. He well knew he could afford no mistakes.

"The first was halved; the match was squared at the second, and on they went, hole after hole, with Sandy playing the same faultless game until 'Pandy' was passed for the last time and Sandy stood two up with only four to go.

"The match looked as good as won—and it was so far as golf was concerned. But, here was the 'Sea Hole' again—and the temper of the Musselburgh men.

"Sure of himself, Sandy placed his drive well to the right in order to play his second along the railing rather than straight toward it. He wasn't taking a chance with any more old boots at that point, and, besides, it was a heady bit of work, if one has the confidence.

"Playing the odd, his ball was on the pin but a trifle hard, stopping safely just over the far side of the green. Chambers, with the utmost care, laid one inside of him on the front of the green but with little advantage, as Sandy's chipping and putting were as steady as a rock.

"Taking his club from the waiting Deacon, he settled in his stance, glanced once at the line, drew back his hands and just as they started forward, something swished through the air and smacked him squarely in the face."

"Aye, by Gawd!" roared Sandy, with a bang of his great fist on the table, that made us all jump. "An' it was naithing else than a dirty, stinkin' fesh th' tide haed swum up an' left. It hit me fair in th' ee an' it smelled awfu'. When I could see, there was a long miner rinnin' awa for th' Gas house. I forgot a' aboot gowf, but I dinna forget ma club; an' I was ower that rail an' smashin' through th' crowd after 'im afore ye could say Jack Robinson.

"There maun hae been a yell, for he gien ae glance ower his shouther, saw me peltin' after 'im wi' ma club, an' rin for his dear life. Around the Gaswork, across Goose Green, past Loretto School he went and taen to th' bank o' th' Esk, makin' for th' brig, thinkin' maybe if he could get across that he'd get awa. But he wudna been safe in hell itsel'; slappin' me in th' face wi' that dirty fesh when I was just makin' ma chip.

"Just afore he come tae th' brig, I come to 'im an' let gang a swipe. Dinna ask me if I tried tae murder 'im; I canna tell—but ma puir club hit on his shouther, instead o' his head, and broke off close tae th' socket. But there was a guid bit o' stout hickory left, an' I gien 'im a threshin' tae last 'im th' rest o' his life." And Sandy, scowling darkly, hid his face behind his pint-stoup for a long, long swallow.

"It must have been nearly a half hour before Sandy returned to finish the match," continued Mr. McPherson. "The balls were still lying where he had left them, his own a few feet on the green where his uncompleted stroke had dribbled it, and Chambers' untouched. But he found the whole place in an uproar, with the Musselburghers led by the miners and no doubt the heaviest bettors, claiming that by running off Sandy had forfeited the match. However, they could not get away with that, and after a great deal of time and argument was wasted, it was decided to go on.

"By then, it was nearing dusk, with a fog drifting in from the sea. Due to the great unmanageable crowd, the deliberation of the champion and the outside interruptions, the round had been slow.

"Sandy had lost a stroke when he was hit, and Chambers, taking no chances, won in a nice four. Still Sandy was one up and three to go.

"In spite of his long run and the general excitement, Sandy halved the next two in par figures; and with all due respect to his own iron nerve, I venture to say the Deacon played no small part in that accomplishment.

"He was just pouring words of wisdom and encouragement into Sandy's ear, when a friendly remark from any of the rest of us might easily have distracted him. Every moment this faithful henchman was right beside him, always with Sandy's own choice of a club held out, when he was not scurrying forward like a ferret to get to the ball and guard it with his life. On the greens, you would see him down on one knee when Sandy was putting, watching that club like a hawk for the slightest faulty movement. A rare 'un among the best, was the Deacon.

"Sandy dormie, one to go, was now cool and confident. Chambers with the honor, and the last hole before him, was a study I shall hardly forget. Defeat stared him in the face, and that on the heels of his championship and on his own home course besides. And here was an opponent who was playing better and sounder golf than he and whom nothing could break.

"That ninth hole is a short one—about 180 yards. In front of the green are two deep bunkers, one on either side, almost closing the entrance, while, all the way from the tee, the ground is rough and irregular. The green itself lays against the inside bend of the race track and is guarded from it by a low railing.

"It takes a grand good shot to find that green and

stay there; but Sandy had just that shot in his bag. Altogether, the hole seemed made for him. But now it was almost dark—too dark for the finish of such an important match.

"The crowd, crazy with excitement, was packed solid around the tee and all the way, both sides of the fairway, to the green where a dense mass was banked clear around it and encroaching upon the green itself.

"Chambers was plainly nervous and for a long time he studied what shot to make, evidently fearing the break if he landed on the slope and ran up, which was what he preferred doing.

"Finally he teed rather high and, taking his favorite Carrick, let go. It was a fine shot for direction but showed his decision to carry all the way, for it was too hard hit. From where I stood on the tee, close beside Sandy, I was certain it would go well over.

"Nevertheless, there was a great shout from that part of the crowd on the green, mingled with some sort of excited yelling whose meaning, in the general noise, was indistinguishable.

"In the midst of a disgraceful racket, Sandy coolly stepped up. One quick glance for the line, and then that clean, crisp hit, perfectly executed for direction and distance. One could see, before the ball was lost to view in the murky darkness, that it was headed straight for the flag and with just the proper length under Sandy's masterful back spin. I tell you, Robert, it takes the Scottish temperament to play golf.

"Another roar broke from the men massed around the green, which increased in volume as we hurried forward. And when we finally pushed and fought our way there, I can only describe it by saying that hell itself had broken loose.

"The crowd was milling and fighting all over the green, down by the railing and out on the track. And there was such a bedlam of yelling and shouting and cursing that at first it was impossible to learn what it was all about.

"Finally we found one ball on the green, close to the flag. It was Chambers'! Sandy's, which we knew had landed fair and would stick, was nowhere to be seen.

"A little impetuous, I daresay, in our excitement, some of us pushed straight through the jeering crowd, shoving them roughly aside in our vain search for the missing ball. By that time it was well on its way to the town; and then we learned how Chambers' ball had been stopped from running clear over on to the track and deliberately kicked back to the hole; while Sandy's, stopping dead, with a fair chance for a two, had been picked up and carried off.

"We were younger then," added Mr. McPherson,

with a reminiscent smile; "and we had not yet acquired that wisdom of control which comes with the years.

"The match, of course, ended there, and I believe Chambers refused to meet Sandy again on more neutral ground. There were no wagers paid—but I fear that some of us took our full toll of satisfaction before we finally left the links and the memory of a visit of the Elie men behind us.

"But what became of you, Sandy?" he inquired abruptly. "I lost sight of both you and the Deacon early in the mêlèe and never set eyes on you again until two days later here in the Elie."

"What became of me!" repeated Sandy in a savage growl. "That thievin' fesh thrower crawled back frae his guid an' proper beatin' an' laid complaint agee me for assault an' battery. They jugged me, they did."

"What!" roared Bob Ferguson.

"That's what they did," reiterated Sandy. "They locked me up in a dirty wee pen; an' I cudna get the smell o' that fesh frae ma hair an' ma face. A' necht through it was awfu'."

It was some minutes before Bob, Miss Jeanie and the minister could control their laughter. Apparently this had been a secret closely guarded by Sandy for the past twenty years.

Another hot toddy—a wee 'Doch an' Dorris,' Bob

[70]

called it—found its way to the table. I felt impelled, as I have said, to express my appreciation to my kindly guests. Then we broke up, and Bob Ferguson courteously accompanied me to the foot of my stairway. It was a fine bit of hospitality.

As I reached my room and prepared for the night, someone was loudly singing:

> *"Hey, ca' through, ca' through,*
> *For we hae mickle ado—ado—"*

I suspect it must have been I.

VI

AFTER what Bob Ferguson truthfully describes as a grand breakfast, I take a long stroll back of Elie, seeking the higher land where the breeze is cool and refreshing.

This Scottish landscape is beautiful with its own peculiar charm—rolling, broken country, generously wooded with large forests or in small, scattered clumps and belts, dotted by innumerable little lakes and ponds and striped with dashing or placid streams.

Some lands are more attractive at a distance; the large scale of their levels and uplands makes for monotony in a close view which does not provide variety in the composition.

On the contrary, I find an intimate glimpse of the Fife country most alluring; and I am sure, on longer acquaintance, every little thicket and stream, field, wood and meadow will become a friend in association with quiet mediation and pleasing companionship.

The peaceful little village of Elie strongly appeals to me. The folk are so straightforward and unaffected, so sincere in their regard. . . .

OUT OF THE ROUGH

I have had a letter from America—and I am considerably disturbed not alone by what it tells me, but as well by the difficulty of analyzing my own response to its disquieting information.

Is it possible that a man can so change with new environment and within the space of two or three weeks? Shrewd Sandy Macgregor called me persistent; I had thought I possessed as well the characteristic of constancy. Yet I cannot deny if this news had been received a fortnight earlier, I would have found myself in far worse affair and probably would have experienced nothing of the sense of anger which seems now my strongest emotion.

I count myself most shabbily disregarded; and the thought obtrudes whether, after all, I have not for the first time merely perceived the actual relation in which I have always been held.

I do not wish to suggest anything derogatory of Angelica, although I could find many expressions which would explain rather than defame. However, such thoughts would be treacherous to the high esteem which constituted my sentiment toward that very lively and attractive young lady—who, I must frankly confess, inspired, if unwittingly, my pilgrimage overseas in quest of the key to the success which held such importance for me.

Who was it that said—'man sees woman only in

the image of his fancy and really knows her not at all'?

Truly—to be frank with myself, for otherwise one shuns honesty—at this moment the fair Angelica does not appear to me the altogether perfect creature I had pictured her at the time when the first obstacles to my ambition in her regard had awakened within me the will to overcome them.

Even now I cannot say this purpose is in anywise weakened by the upsetting news which came to me this morning. Quite on the contrary, I am more than ever resolved to accomplish my aim to become a sound and proficient golfer.

The impulse underlying my determination had been purely a desire to win her approval. I am not altogether sure that such admirable sentiment is now unmixed with a wish for revenge—a rather potent ingredient at that.

At the least, I shall remain constant in my intention, and no matter how strong the impulse to hurry back and view the situation from near, I shall resist it and put my plan to the test. And if I achieve success, time alone will show to what end my accomplishment will serve me. . . .

A keen and sound philosopher, Mr. McPherson. He has, too, a perfect comprehension of the proper mental attitude toward golf. He stated, as I now recollect it, that temperament is a most important

[74]

factor, controlling the disastrous effects of nervousness or overeagerness. Essentially, one must have poise. Therefore, I shall try resolutely to put from my mind all thought of that abominable letter—at least until I have had my lesson of this afternoon.

I cross a slope of purple heather, climb a bold rock and gaze backward beyond the moorland and the quaint, old roofs of Elie; beyond the gleaming, placid water that is the Firth of Forth; further still where a light mist softly swathes the rugged headlands of the coast.

This freeing one's mind of annoying subjects is not such an easy task. My thoughts outdistance the vision of my eye and essay to fly beyond the brown cliffs, further, across the wide ocean that separates me from their destination.

Borne on the swift wings of fancy, I see the well kept fairways and greens of Folothru, the large, pretentious club-house with its spacious verandas filled with an eager, restless throng, the laughing, somewhat mocking little crowd at the starting place as we tee up and are away.

I am playing a foursome with Angelica as a partner. It is the last and one of the very few games I have ever enjoy—er—I have ever had with her.

Our opponents are a Miss Somebody-or-other and Dick Hilton. I see him very clearly, for it seemed to me he paid Angelica the attention he should have reserved for his own partner—and Angelica appeared quite content.

I do not linger upon the torture of that round. My game at all times was bad enough. I made no pretentions at Folothru; everyone knew it. But I have always thought it might not have been quite so awful if I had received even a slight measure of encouragement, or at least been spared a most obvious if silent reproach.

We come to the eighteenth tee, finishing the unconsoling bye holes. My drive slices off to the rough. I was thankful to get away at all; but I hasten along beside Angelica, proffering my best apologies. She strides along, with that quick, characteristic step, silent until the ball is eventually found.

She studies it a moment with a vexed frown, smiles over at that detestable Dick Hilton who waves a commiserating hand—he lies a hundred yards further on, in the fairway—snaps a heavy mashie from the bag and, settling in her stance, addresses to me almost her first words of the afternoon:

"What a really hopeless duffer you are, Bobbie!"

Of course her recovery is superb. A perfectly timed stroke, carried all the way through, that leaves her poised in graceful posture until the ball lands safely on the course.

Hilton applauds. She hurries forward to join him. . . .

Out of the Rough

Hang it all! Confound that letter anyway!

My mind reverts to the present. My gaze comes back from the gray mist curtain and falls on the sweet land before me. I turn and descend, striving desperately to divert my attention from its rather distracting contemplation.

It seems that my step must have kept pace with my racing thoughts, for, before I am quite aware of it, I find myself again in a quiet lane of Elie; and turning an abrupt corner of a thick hedge, I come face to face with a vision so charming I am conscious of an unaccountable little thrill of pleasure.

"Guid mornin'!" greets Miss Jeanie with a laugh and a bright smile. "Losh, man! ye fair startled me, burstin' frae that wynd like a Jack-in-the-box."

"Good morning to you, Miss Jeanie," I return with a feeling of friendliness in spite of the dignity which becomes a guest at her father's inn. "How wonderfully—er—fresh you look! Not a bit tired by our long dinner last evening."

"Fegs, an' why not?" she answers, with her little head atilt and one brown eye mocking me from under the wide brim of her hat. "Ye a' were sic guid friends wi' th' ale, while I hardly took a wee sippie." Then she breaks into gay, ringing laughter. "Ye hae worked a miracle, mister Hale. For as lang as I can remember, they hae tried to mak Sandy tell the story of his match at Musselbur-ra, but never would he say a word ava. I laughed the whole necht through."

We are walking side by side down the bordered lane. I take from her the large basket she is carrying, and observe it holds empty pots and dishes.

"You have been out on an errand?" I ask a little blankly, for really the fresh, modest beauty of this girl is quite disturbing. She glances at me in keen amusement.

"Oh—aye; I hae been servin' a meal. 'Tis puir auld Grannie Robertson. She lives a' alane an' hae been ailin' an' canna weel dae things for hersel'."

"I expect your kindness of heart as well as your duty urged you to do it."

At which she again laughs merrily.

"Dae ye like th' Elie, mister Hale? It is such a puir, sleepy little place, a grand man like ye maun find in't naithing of great interest." Her sweet, low voice drawls a little as she says it; and a glance shows me her bright eyes sparkling mischievously.

"Oh—to me it is altogether charming and picturesque. Everything in it is so peaceful and—er—beautiful. And all the people I have met are so kind and friendly. Are they always like that to a stranger?"

We have now come before the Inn, and I hold out her basket. As she takes it from me, she meets my glance for a moment, and in that brief instant she is

[78]

not smiling and I perceive how wonderfully deep and warm her brown eyes can be.

"I maun gae tae the Manse yonder." She turns a little; then glances back over her shoulder. "It is, mister Hale, because they a' think ye are a guid man and dinna put on the grand airs wi' the simple folk."

A bright smile dimples her face and lights her dark eyes as she hurries away. . . .

My headache of the morning was left on the moorland, and greatly refreshed by my walk and Bob's stout luncheon, I set out for Sandy's in high spirits, speculating, to be sure, in what humor I shall find him.

When I round the corner of his snug cottage, I perceive him sitting in the doorway of his shop, and quite filling it at that. He is smoking his favorite pipe and appears engrossed in meditation. I wonder how these quiet folk find so much to think about.

As he catches sight of me, his expression instantly brightens—which to my eager mind is like the appearance of a rainbow of most auspicious hue—an augury of good nature suited to my purpose.

"Ah, Robert, man," is his hearty greeting; "I hae lang been waitin' for ye, laddie. We hae muckle work afore us an' we maun gang tae't."

There is a certain characteristic of humankind

[79]

that renders all men prone to gratification at the attention of some notable personage. Since the days of the phlegmatic Diogenes, I doubt if any man has lived who was not susceptible to this weakness, although, to be sure, some fortune-favored ones pretend at least to look high for this impulse. As for me, who in my modest way have not passed altogether unnoticed, I do not believe I have ever experienced greater satisfaction than I now derive from the friendly attitude of this dour Scotsman whose taciturnity is a byword among his neighbors. Silently I wait for his next words.

Sitting forward in his chair, with his pipe poised for emphasis, Sandy fixes me with his keen, twinkling eyes whose expression is at first puzzling.

"Mony a man," he continued, "mak's idle boast when his skin is tight wi' the guid liquor he has poured in't. I dinna say, Robert, we haed ower muckle yester e'en; but I ken weel I hae made a match for ye wi' th' minister wha's a canny man wi' his clubs in spite o' his religion. In a fortnecht, laddie, I can tell ye a' there is tae gowf but ye wudna play ane stroke better unless ye pay heed an' dae exactly as I show ye."

I assure him, with considerable enthusiasm, that to obey his instructions to the letter was the sole purpose which has brought me such a great distance to the little town of Elie.

[80]

"Verra weel, Robert, if ye wudna shame me afore the villagers, listen wi' your lugs maist carefu' an' let your ain ideas gang a' agley.

"Ye ken the head maun stay still, which keeps th' body frae swaying and humping up and doun. Remember it!

"I hae tauld ye how th' arms swing free o' themsel's withoot being pulled through by th' shouthers, an' the club gaes in tae th' ba' like th' swingle o' th' threshin'-tree.

"That, Robert, is th' main secret and principle o' th' gowf stroke. Tae dae it is th' thing ye maun learn; an' I tell ye, laddie, it is th' maist simple thing in th' warl' if ye heed weel an' nae let yoursel' dae itherwise.

"Noo——" In his earnestness, Sandy rises from his chair and steps closer to me—— "This mair ye maun understaund. Th' han's an' th' arms gang through a wide circle. Tae permit them tae travel, th' body turns on a pivot.

"Get that clear in your mind, Robert. 'Tis a pivoting o' th' body tae allow th' arms dae their work properly. It is not a swing o' th' body tae pull them through after. Dae ye understaund that, laddie?"

"A pivot and not a swing of the body," I repeat. "The arms lead through and the club is whipped into the ball like the end stick of the flail."

"Robert!" Sandy points his pipe at me. "If ye

keep that alane always in mind—everra stroke ye mak—ye'll be a gowfer!"

The seriousness of his manner impresses me as no other instruction I have ever received, no matter what the subject. I fully realize that at last the secret of the stroke, which had so completely baffled me, is being made clear in a way I thoroughly comprehend. I vow to myself, over again, I will in every way do exactly as he tells me.

Evidently he is satisfied with my expression which I daresay is grim with determination. He turns toward the shop and, reaching inside the doorway, produces a driver.

"Th' day, Robert, we'll concentrate anely on th' pivot. Staund there, wi' your feet apart—nae sae far, laddie; nae sae far. Be easy, th' noo; feel your weight on baith legs, Robert, but mair on your recht, an' frae the ba' o' your foot tae th' heel. Never rock on your tiptaes. So—wi' your taes straight, an' sort o' grippin' th' grun wi' th' inside o' your feet. Your shouthers can fa' natural, but ye maun stick oot th' end o' your spine tae balance their weight.

"Noo, steady on your balance, tak th' club in your han's an' grip it just firm enough tae control an' guide it and sae it winna shift, for ye maun always remember your twa hands are a fixed pairt o' th' club an' th' bend o' your wrists is like th' cord that binds th' swingle tae th' handle o' th' threshin'-tree.

"Let your hands hang doun natural an' rest th'
club on th' grun. Dinna bend way forrard tae
reach for't. Noo—we'll gang verra, verra slow at
first."

Sandy steps in front of me and, stooping, takes
hold of the shaft with a light touch.

"Tae start, Robert, bend your left knee in toward
th' recht. Guid! Noo ye perceive your han's hae
started back by themsel's. Ye'll also see your hips
hae turned, an' your shouthers are gaun tae follow
a' recht. As ye gang further, raise your left heel a
wee bit tae mak it easier; and tak notice th' club
head is travelin' in tae your recht, which is th' course
it maun follow when it comes doun again.

"Noo—keep your han's gaun back wi' th' left arm
straight. Dinna think o' liftin' th' club. It'll gae up
itsel' if ye keep on gaun. Mak your body an' shouthers pivot on the centre, wi' th' left shouther gaun
under, doun toward th' ba'. Dinna swing yoursel'
around back. That's high eneugh for your han's th'
noo, Robert. It's th' top o' your backswing.

"Noo—twist your knees back an' feel th' club start
doun wi' th' pull on your left arm. Never mind th'
flick o' th' wrist th' noo—ye're gaun slow. Wi' your
head still, watch how th' club head will travel frae
your recht, through th' ba' and oot as far as it'll
gang.

"Keep your recht elbow close tae ye an' dinna let

[83]

your wrist turn ower till it's past the ba'. Mind your pivot an' let your recht shouther gang under th' noo —slow——— Weel done, Robert. Ance mair."

Sandy keeps me at this slow pivoting, with a patience that amazes me, until I see clearly in my mind just how the club head should travel and exactly how my hands and arms and body must act to accomplish it. The movements, of course, are very leisurely and without any force, but after a while they attain a certain symmetry that is a revelation to me who had gathered all the faults the worst duffer could possess.

What impresses me more than any other one thing is, imagining a ball opposite my left heel, the club head approaches the spot from inside its flight-line at my right, goes through it and on for a little distance until my extended arms bring it around.

"Noo, Robert," remarks Sandy, "when ye hae mastered that, the club head will hit the ba' true an' straight everra time, an' it is the ane way in a' the warl' it can be done."

Sandy is silent a moment, as if to allow this maxim to sink home; then resumes:

"A slice comes when th' club head is drawn across th' ba' frae outside th' line an' sharply in tae your left. Gie me the club, while ye rest a wee bit, and I'll show ye how that can happen.

"If th' shouthers start first and pull the hands

after, it daes it. See? That is a swing o' the body and not a pivot.

"If your recht shouther comes around on a level wi' your left, it turns your whole body tae the left an' daes it. This can also happen if ye draw your left arm in.

"When the club gangs through, if your weight has not gaen forrard tae your firm left leg, ye'll perceive th' club head is again drawn in tae your left— which daes it.

"There is mair tae be said on this same subject, but those three things, Robert, ye maun avoid as ye would the deil himsel'."

VII

THIS, I tell myself, has been my first real lesson with a golf club in my hands and trying to execute the movements which old Sandy Macgregor made so understandable to me.

I am filled with elation to realize at last I have taken the first if tottering steps along the only path which leads to expertness in this very elusive art; and on my way back to the Inn, I am utterly unconscious of my surroundings or of whom I chance to meet, in my absorption over the several fundamental points which Sandy has imparted to me from his store of golden knowledge.

In my mind, as I walk along, I go over them again, wishing to fix them all clearly in order to practice correctly:

The proper distribution of weight on my feet and keeping it back on the heels, giving the firm balance.

Commencing the upswing by bending my left knee in toward the right, which, turning my hips, starts the pivot, bringing my left shoulder round and down and thus carrying my hands to the right.

Taking the club back with a straight left arm, *my*

[86]

right elbow in close and a firm grip with both hands
—head still.

Then I think of the actual stroke, as Sandy has so
far explained it to me, with an exceedingly slow motion so that I may comprehend each separate movement. Probably what he has told me today is only
elementary and he will have much more to add and
explain before I can learn how each part should work
and make the stroke with one swift, even flowing
motion.

First, then, the dont's:

Don't start the shoulders and the body into the
stroke, pulling the arms and the club after.

Now it is plain to me that this was exactly the way
in which I had always hit at the ball, conceiving it
some heavy obstacle which should be clouted with all
the strength of my back and shoulders.

Indeed, I am fortunate to have found such a
teacher as Sandy Macgregor who makes his points
clear by the greatest method of all—that of understandable, homely simile. With his fly-casting and
the action of the flail, he has made me see the utter
fallacy of this blind exertion of brute force.

"It's the swingle that beats the grain from the
wheat; the tap of the club head which sends the ball
away!"

A swing of the body will not accomplish this—any
more than a sweep of the full arm will cast a fly—

[87]

for then there's no flick of wrist, and club and the head do not come up from behind and hit squarely. Therefore, the second don't:

The right shoulder must follow the hand under, and not come around on a level with the left. The whole body action must be a *pivot* merely, and not a *swing*.

I shall make careful analysis of the difference between these two; since right here, it now appears to me, lies the crux of my whole affair, deciding whether or not I can succeed in throwing off my old abominable faults and start playing the stroke in the only proper way. A *pivot* and not a *swing*, with the body muscles loose, and a feeling of effort in the arms alone.

The third warning he gave me was to be certain that the weight of the body, on the pivot through, goes to the firm left leg.

I wonder if my ignorance of that explains why I invariably finished my most vicious swings with my left foot dragged around and my whole body bent backward and away from the direction in which I fondly hoped the ball was traveling.

From the top of the backswing, I must start the stroke with a sense of pulling down with my left arm. Then the hands will surely lead and the pivoting shoulders follow.

So—thus the wrists flail out the club as the body

[88]

pivots, and the club head, from inside to the right, travels through the ball and on along that line as far as the arms, with the right shoulder under, permit. . . .

At this point in my intent musing, I reach my room and, impelled by my hot enthusiasm, I take out a driver, set myself before the mirror I have arranged for the purpose, and slowly repeat, over and over, this stroke which in all its features is so new to me.

After a time, I move to one side where I cannot see my reflection and, as a consequence, keep my head down where it properly belongs during the stroke.

"Hands first, right shoulder *pivoting* under and after, weight going to the firm left leg, the club whipped through and out," I repeat aloud, suiting action to word.

And now I am sensible of the fact that I am subjecting myself to a moral as well as physical lesson.

I am absolutely determined to master the game. I have tried once and many times and failed dismally. On the right track at last and with no questionings or misgivings, I shall make my body and limbs learn their functions through habit of constant practice.

In two weeks, Sandy says, I am to play a match with the genial Mr. McPherson. As I drop my driver into the bag, I feel that I shall not discredit him. . . .

OUT OF THE ROUGH

The light is beginning to fail. I have been at it longer than I realized; but far from begrudging the time spent upon these simple fundamental exercises without once hurrying the stroke, I am more content than since I first conceived this wonderful plan.

I am confident I shall surprise my friends—and those other better players who rarely deigned to look at my game.

I have observed that golfers are not unlike a well dressed woman in the respect that neither vouchsafe a second glance at one beneath his standard. Before I became aware of this rather commiserating truth, I was most reluctant to make a stroke with anyone around. Now all that will be different. Quite! From a thirty—the maximum handicap of the hopeless duffers—I shall work my way at once into more respected company.

I light my lamp and the idea occurs to me to get out a card of the Folothru first eighteen—the championship course, by Jove!—and set a score, hole by hole, to equal or improve upon when I shall play it on my return. It is well to have a mark at which to aim, and I am justified in my ambition.

As I rummage through a drawer of my dresser, I come upon an envelope which pulls me up with a sudden start and a certain feeling of dismay.

Although this morning it had driven me to a long, rapid walk over the moorland and sent all my best thoughts ascatter, I had completely forgotten its existence in the presence of other affairs. By Jove! I have not once thought of the whole detestable business since I met Miss Jeanie in the lane. Now, that is strange.

I take out the letter with a grim smile and decide to read it again for the sole purpose of judging its present effect upon me.

A few hours earlier it had struck me with a sense of calamity, knocking the bedrock of my purpose from beneath my feet. I am quite calm now as I unfold the several sheets and seat myself by the light.

Of course I had no other thought with reference to this rather intimate communication than to burn it forthwith. When I commenced these notes (to which, if the end justifies it, I shall probably give some such encouraging title as "Out of the Rough," or "The Triumph of a Duffer") I made very clear my aversion to the exploitation of one's own private affairs.

To explain the conception of my somewhat unique plan, I implied its cause; and to be consistent, I expect it is my duty to omit nothing of material influence upon my progress to the coveted goal. In this, I am well entrenched; since success alone will ever bring my jottings before the eyes of any other, and in that event, through my sympathy for my fellows in perplexity I would deny them nothing.

The letter is from one of my few intimate friends, Harold Bosworth.

A steady, decent sort of chap is Harold; but, as one will readily perceive, he lacks proper regard for another's sensibilities. He is too brutally frank.

"Dear Blimp":

(I dislike that nickname exceedingly. As a matter of fact, I was not in that branch of the artillery.)

"To run away is generally accepted as an admission of guilt. It also advertises a motive which, theretofore, may not have been suspected.

"Of course, I was aware you were hard hit"—(an assumption I shall not readily overlook, even from Bosworth)—"but to flee by stealth to parts unknown and allow your best friends the futile agony of endeavoring to extract the slightest suspicion of information from that wooden headed man of yours, argue an attempted engagement with utter defeat and rout.

"Sorry, old man. Hope it won't embitter your gay young life and make of jolly old Hale a bore of a gloomy misanthrope." (Stupid ass!)

"But even that doesn't excuse your shabby treatment of your friends. Three times I called your rooms by telephone only to be told: 'Mr. 'ale his hout!' Then I inquired in person and elicited the same intelligent response.

" 'All right,' says I, 'I'll wait. Give me something from the cabinet and set out a box of Bobbie's best

[92]

Havanas.' I had just finished a fervid round and felt the need of relaxation.

" 'Hi wery much fear, sir, you'll 'ave long to wait, sir,' answers your Paragon. 'Hand besides, sir, heverything his hall locked hup!'

"And that's all the dumb-bell would tell me under bribe and threat. I was so peeved, I'd jolly well spare myself the trouble of writing you at all if it were not for a bit of news that should thrill your callous soul.

"On the second fruitless day, I gave the matter thought and promptly arrived at the logical conclusion; and, as evidence of my profound friendship for one so little deserving, I at once decided to make the affair my own—in your interest, of course. You can be assured I have no wish to star as John Alden."

(Friend or not, I should like to wring his infernal neck.)

"So I sought out the lady in the case and skilfully approached the subject.

"Had she seen you at the club that day? She thought so, but wasn't quite certain—'there are always so many men around.' And that without the flicker of one mascaraed eyelash!

"It somewhat nettled me—as attorney for the absent plaintiff, keep in mind—so I informed her I had excellent reason to believe you had gone somewhere and drowned yourself or indulged in some such trivial recklessness.

[93]

" 'How provoking,' she replies, with a cool stare at me. 'Bobbie is quite useful—away from the links.'

"Sorry if it hurts, old man; but the bitterest truth is the speediest panacea, you know.

"In consequence, becoming more angry, as a good friend was bound to, I suggested that she knew very well the circumstance and cause of your abrupt and mysterious disappearance—for which she bade me not be stupid and challenged me to a ten dollar Nassau, even.

"After all, we had a jolly match. She is keen and a ripping good sport; conceded me putts I would not have given to a man. I took the first nine, one up, and when we finished the sixteenth all square, she suggested doubling.

"I paid her twenty for my complacence. It was well worth it, old boy. But how any girl can play winning bridge or golf and talk while doing it is one of the mysteries of creation. I do not mean she talked me out of it—she's too square for that—simply that man is not made to concentrate when woman's charming prattle falls upon his ear. I expect it's the instinct of gallantry inherent in the sex.

"But she's interesting company, is Angelica; a winner if one has the brightness of intellect to match her pace. I can now thoroughly understand your admiration. She quite roused me out of myself and, from first hole to last, we had a most brilliant exchange of repartee—a most enjoyable afternoon, by gad!

"And what a sport she is! It's a fad of this mad day, I expect—and every girl eager to outdo all others.

"Take Angelica. Since you have voluntarily withdrawn from the lists, old fellow, we can of course discuss her impersonally. She is one of the prizes of her set—looks, I'll say, money, family, exceptional intelligence for a girl, as I remarked, good dancer and a splendid golfer. She's mad about golf—her hobby and she rides it to perfection.

"Do not flatter yourself you were the only one with a discriminating eye. There are Dick Hilton, Bernie Evans and perhaps a dozen others; but Dick and Bernie are the leaders and running neck and neck.

"I'm loyal, old bird, and would still back you if you had the ghost of a chance; but since you yourself put the that's that on it, we might as well glimpse the field.

"Pretty evenly matched, those two, in ways I expect a woman sees. Neither has your Rolls Royce, although they may possess other compensating appeal to the womanly eye. And you are scratched.

"Apparently Angelica herself finds difficulty in drawing a line between them and both are prime favorites—quick talkers, fast actors and—keen golfers. They're both '6' men, you know. Best in the club.

"So—here's her sporting proposition. I'll give it to you in one lump. You can swallow it quicker that way.

"Namely—the hand and heart and altogether adorable personage of Miss Angelica go to the winner of the club championship to be played at scratch this Fall!

"Can you beat that for downright sporting nerve!

"I must admit, at first I was rudely shocked—as I can take my oath you are. In the last few days of more intimate acquaintance—we have been playing a rubber match—I had formed a very high opinion of her, and this sort of thing struck me with a suggestion of immoral recklessness.

"However, on more sober thought—to which I recommend you—I perceived my error and more credit to Miss Angelica's perspicacity.

"This is not a maiden's heart to be given away at the flick of a coin. It is the weighing of two characters by the most drastic and fairest test conceivable.

"To be sure, golf is a game—in a sort of way. But at that, it is a shrewd determinator of the quality in a man.

"These chaps, both likable fellows, are evenly matched in skill. Barring the ordinary run of luck, it seems plausible to me that he who conducts himself more admirably under such trying circumstances,

[96]

will exhibit the greater self control and thus prove his superior suitability as a husband of this most charming and terribly energetic young lady.

"All honor to the keen intuition and the sporting blood of Angelica, say I!

"Of course, Folothru is frightfully fussed over it, and the society columns have much to say, properly and profusely illustrated.

"Some safely married o. l's. appealed to the governors in protest and were even about to request her withdrawal from the club; but we men folk rose up *en masse* and proclaimed the sportingness of the proposition, so the affair is definitely on.

"Everyone concedes that the match lies between Evans and Hilton; yet that fact has not deterred all other unattached male creatures from entering, to give it suitable *éclat* and to take a long chance on the big money.

"My name is in and I added yours, with the thoughtful idea, which I trust you will duly appreciate, that in this way you can best show the jolly world what a good loser you are."

(For which I thank you, friend Bosworth, and shall most assuredly punch your fat head on the first available opportunity.)

"Angelica takes it all with becoming coolness—the grand fanfare in the papers and the rest. This very morning I observed her examining the long list of entries, and I give you my word she laughed until the tears trespassed upon her freshly glowing cheeks. Some poesy, that.

"So there you are, old bean; but where you are, God and this simpleton of yours only know and I cannot discover.

"I am entrusting this to the care of your Bosche headed man. The responsibility yours, if it does not find you in time and bring you back to the keenest sporting event of these hectic days.

"Ta-ta and too-ra-loo, old dear.

Yours in the spirit of conquest,

H. B."

VIII

"NOO," begins Sandy the following afternoon, "ye canna get the whole beuk in ae chapter, Robert.

"There are twa eesential pairts tae th' gowf stroke. Tane is th' manner in which ye hauld yer club an' yersel'; tither is th' way ye put force in't.

"So far I hae gien ye a wee glimpse at baith tae-gither, for ye are a thinkin' man an' would ken how th' biggit house'll leuk while we work on th' pairts that mak it."

A bit of a philosopher, this rough old Sandy Macgregor. And I have already observed that the more I study to get the meaning of his words and a full conception of his sayings, the clearer and more definite become the various impressions in my mind. It is largely for that reason that I am quoting him exactly in the words he speaks to me.

If one reads a certain subject glancingly and does not follow the explanations with careful thought, or again if one listens to an instructor with half a mind, the other being engaged meanwhile with questions of his own making, it is obvious that little benefit will be derived therefrom.

To employ a homely simile—by chance and good fortune I have found a rare specialist in the disorders which affected my game of golf, and I am acutely conscious that ninety per cent of the efficacy of his cure lies in my own application of it.

To receive this cure, I have come a long ways overseas and being if not an impoverished at least a practical American, I am bound to get the best there is in it.

Very carefully I am making comprehensive notes of the various points Sandy gives me as I go on, which I both study and practice consistently when I am alone. While he is talking, however, I am schooling myself to think of nothing but the explanations he is making.

"Yester," he continues, "I hae showed ye the path th' club head maun travel in order tae hit th' ba' fair an' square an' gie ye a straight shot. An' ye saw how yer arms maun move tae dae it. But ye did it verra slow, wi'oot force or snap tae 't, sae tae see th' different movements fer yersel'.

"We'll noo gang ower th' same grun and a little further, an' tak up th' second pairt o' th' question, how tae gie force tae th' stroke, in its proper place.

"First comes th' grip, an' this starts a question which I hae na doot'll be fecht ower as long as gowf is played. It's whether the left han' or the recht han' has mair tae dae; an' I'll answer it thilka way.

"Maist men canna twist th' body lithely; also, tae get a square hit an' nae a slice, the club head maun gang oot wi' th' ba' an' nae draw across it."

Sandy steps to a bare spot of earth and marks the position of his feet in the stance and also the point where the club head would lie against the teed ball.

"Noo ye see, Robert, when I hauld th' driver in my recht hand alane and swing it wi'out turnin' ma shouther doun, it mak's a short circle like this." He traces a short arc in the sand. "And when I hauld it in my left alane, it gangs through th' ba' and oot a guid foot further.

"Tae mak th' recht han' travel near th' same line the left has gaen, yer recht shouther maun gang awa doun and oot which maist men canna dae easily.

"Therefore, I tell ye tae hauld yer club firm in yer left hand an' guide it and push it mair wi' the fingers o' yer recht, keeping in mind tae get yer recht shouther doun an' oot forrard as far as ye are able.

"I dinna want tae confuse ye, Bobbie, but recht here is th' crux o' th' whole matter, an' ye maun hae it clear in yer mind.

"Listen—— When th' recht shouther turns doun toward th' ba', th' left shouther maun turn awa frae it. Yer two han's are taegither; therefore, ye maun hit a compromise atween baith, sae that baith will carry th' club head oot beyond th' line, an' nae ane or tither pull it in across that line.

"An' recht here I'll tell ye tae keep yer baith elbows doun an' in, frae th' stance an' through a' pairts o' th' stroke. That is maist important fer a man inclined tae slice th' ba'.

"Noo, fer th' grip: Place yer left thumb back o' the shaft and doun it, an' hauld th' club in yer fingers an' palm. That thumb'll gie ye purchase. Noo place yer recht little finger around yer left forefinger. Yer recht palm gaes on top and ower yer left thumb an' th' club lies easily between th' lower knuckles o' yer recht thumb an' forefinger.

"Noo yer left hand'll hauld th' club an' yer recht fingers 'll guide an' push it, which is proper.

"Ye hae kept in mind, Robert, that the bendin' o' th' wrists is like th' cord o' th' threshin-tree. Sae, by haulding yer hands close taegither, ye get th' bendin' at ane point an' nae at twa, or ane hand or tither'll tak th' club a' tae itsel'.

"Mak yer backswing th' noo as I showed ye yester —verra slow."

I comply and, aided by the practice I have taken meanwhile, I feel confident that I make no mistake.

"Ye maun get a' th' muscles o' yer upper body loose, Robert, sae yer left shouther'll come doun mair on th' upswing. If ye tauten th' body an' shouther muscles ye canna dae it, and I'll mak that a'

[102]

clear tae ye when we come tae put power in th' stroke. Noo, doun an' watch how th' club head travels. Let it gang oot—wi' th' recht shouther way under."

Slowly, back and forth, I trail the club a dozen or perhaps a score of times until I am aware that a certain smoothness and regularity have come into the movements.

Then to my surprise, Sandy stops me and takes the driver from my hands.

"We'll dae na mair here th' day, Robert. Ye can practice that at hame by yersel' till ye hae clear in yer mind th' picture of how everything gaes. An' ye mauna forget tae keep baith those elbows in."

Sandy sets the club in his shop and rejoining me draws out his pipe and commences leisurely to fill it. As he sets a match to the tobacco, he looks at me with eyes that twinkle.

"Dinna fash yersel' aboot th' troubles o' th' game o' gowf, laddie. Why, man, yer face is as serious as an owl. Gowf is a' fun, an' while I'll nae say at times it's nae verra tryin' on th' deesposition, it's nae th' disagreeable work some mak o't.

"Noo, we'll gang ower tae th' links an' hae a keek at th' minister at work. He's oot fer practice th' day agee his match wi' ye. We might learn something."

I light my own pipe as we walk on.

"I hae seen by th' leuk in yer ee, Robert," continues Sandy after a moment, "when ye hae first taen th' club, that ye are feart o' something an' that ye were in grand haste tae hit th' ba' afore it could get awa frae ye."

He smokes on for a little while in silence which I do not care to break.

"I hae seen, too, that ye hae played a bit, an' na doot," he adds shrewdly, "ye're worrit ower a' th' faults ye've haed. Ye can forget a' that, laddie. We're gaun tae mak ye a new stroke frae th' beginning an' ye'll hae naught tae think of that ye ever haed afore.

"Many's th' pupil I've haed. Yon minister's ane. And it's verra important fer th' instructor tae study his pupil afore ever he tries tae teach him something. Some men hae nae th' head tae compreehend gowf if ye talk tae 'em frae th' noo till th' day o' doom. Then there's ithers wha'll never listen, and still ithers sae stubborn they'll never agree ye're recht.

"Th' minister, ower there, is a fine man; there's nae better—as a man. But he's a wee bit odd when it comes tae gowf. He compreehends th' theory o' th' game an' kens verra weel th' philosophy o' human nature, but he'll hae his ain way wi' his strokes in spite o' th' deil himsel'."

By this time we have come on the links, and Sandy stops beside the broad green of the seventeenth, as I observe from the figure "18" on a nearby tee-box. Directly as we face, beyond a narrow strip of gorse,

[104]

the long sixteenth fairway runs past us to the right where we can see a portion of the well trapped green. At some distance to the left, two players are coming along the fifteenth. In one, I recognize the tall, powerful figure of Mr. McPherson. A girl is walking beside him, with a club in her hand.

In silence, Sandy watches them approach and putt out. Mr. McPherson leads the way to the next tee.

"An' that's ae reason," continues Sandy, as if unconscious of the interval since he last spoke, "why I hae na gien 'im a' I ken aboot gowf. Ye ken, Robert, that there's ane recht way aboot th' proper playin' o' th' stroke. Ye can watch th' best gowfers an' ye'll never see it. Many's the man that haes it an' dinna kens it, an' there's still mair wha canna explain it proper.

"Noo, watch th' minister drive, Robert, an' see what ye'll hae o't."

A distance of perhaps one hundred yards separates us from the sixteenth tee. Mr. McPherson does not tarry over his shot and it seems to me that his form is good. His follow through is particularly fine and he finishes firmly on his feet. I am not surprised that his drive, while not directly on the line and a trifle high, is easily over two hundred yards.

"Weel?"

"He puts lots of power into it," I answer hesitantly.

"That he daes," agrees Sandy dryly. "Noo leuk at Jeanie."

"Miss Jeanie!" I gasp in great amazement. "Miss ____"

"Watch, laddie, watch!"

And watch I do.

Even at that distance, I marvel at the consummate ease and smoothness of her rather full stroke. In fact I am so engrossed in my observation and wonder that she should be Mr. McPherson's partner that I do not follow the ball after the sharp, crisp click that comes to us clearly on the still air. Decidedly, this daughter of the innkeeper is a rather extraordinary young person.

"Weel, dae ye observe any deeference?" asks Sandy, interrupting my surprised musing.

"I see a great difference," I reply, a little puzzled, "but I can't tell you exactly what it is. He comes through cleanly and hits a very hard ball. Her stroke is so easily made, she doesn't seem to put enough effort in it to get distance. Her form to me is remarkable. Of course they were some way off, but I am quite certain I have never seen another girl drive like that."

It is true. I had thought Angelica one of the best players of her sex; but her stroke is quick and with a display of considerable effort, while that of this Scottish lassie I can best describe as the embodiment

[106]

of ease. And yet from her appearance, her straight, erect figure, her light, springy stride, I should judge she is much the stronger of the two.

The players, chatting pleasantly together, come opposite, wave their hands and smile.

"Wait and go in with us," calls Mr. McPherson.

"With pleasure," I shout back.

Sandy is stolidly smoking his pipe, with never a word or a nod, although I feel with curious reluctance that her smile is for him. However, I observe his keen eyes are very bright as he watches them go on to their balls.

That of Mr. McPherson lies well over to the left and, to my surprise, he reaches for a club while Miss Jeanie stops and waits for him to make the shot.

"What!" I exclaim involuntarily. "You mean to say he's playing the odd?"

Sandy chuckles.

"But—he must have been over two hundred!"

"Aboot twa hunner an' twalve an' hooked a guid bit off th' line. Miss Jeanie lies ten yards further an' straight as a string fer th' pin."

In silent amazement I watch their irons. It is plain that Mr. McPherson has the strength and he uses it generously. Quite a bit of turf starts with the ball which, this time, carries to the right of the flag. A very creditable shot it seems to me.

Again Miss Jeanie plays with that perfect symmctry of smoothness which, I am convinced, disguises the real effort in the stroke. From the crisp sound, it is unquestionably a clean, hard hit, and I see the ball bounce once on the near side of the distant green. I do not watch their putts as Sandy is speaking again.

"Noo dae ye understaund it?" he inquires.

"You mean—how she gets such distance with so little apparent effort? No, I'm hanged if I do!"

"An' ye wudna. Yet, before yer ee, in th' play o' th' twa, ye haed it shown ye fair an' clear."

"Miss Jeanie—knows this idea you spoke of, Sandy?"

"Aye, she kens it recht weel. And I'll na say th' minister haes nae been told o't. But he's a bit stubborn as I was tellin' ye, and it's na use tae force a stubborn man!"

"And——" I begin and stop.

"Aye, laddie; I'm gaun tae explain it tae ye afore ever ye hit a ba'. Ye're mindin' weel what I tell ye, an' there's th' match wi' the minister, when na doot half th' Elie'll come over tae see't. Noo watch them come tae th' green. It's nae a lang shot an' they'll baith tak mashies, but Miss Jeanie'll play hers lower an' it'll hauld it—see?"

And truly, the ball, rising not so high as I should have thought a mashie would pitch it, lands on the narrow entrance to the green, takes a short bounce with a little run and fetches up about ten feet from the pin.

"But, Sandy," I demand, "how does she manage to get such direction? I have not the least notion in what manner one plays for accuracy."

"That," returns Sandy slowly, as we both watch Mr. McPherson take his stance, "is ane o' the verra important results o' this idea o' mine. I'll gie ye something tae think ower th' necht, Robert. 'Tis this—th' muscles that gie th' power tae th' stroke canna dae guid work at guidin'. Dae ye understaund?"

"The muscles that give the stroke its power cannot at the same time be depended upon to control the direction of the shot," I mechanically repeat, trying to fix this unusual postulation in my mind for further consideration.

"That, laddie, should gie ye th' key tae it a'. But nae be discouraged if ye dinna guess it. Many a man haes thought himsel' gray in th' head ower this same subject. Noo, there gaes th' minister's ba', reachin' fer th' clouds, an' wi' luck he'll land somewhere near on. And if he nae haes luck an' maks th' trap, he'll gang doun oot o' secht."

But luck is with him and his ball stops not far from Miss Jeanie's, to the accompaniment of a hearty shout from the jovial clergyman as the two of them hasten on toward us.

Now, it is quite difficult for me to express, as it

would be to analyze my exact feelings, as I stand watching Miss Jeanie approach with that free, swinging stride that is so typical of her.

I am not ashamed to confess that I have never seen a fairer picture than she presents at this moment. Her cheeks are flushed from the healthful exercise; little wisps and curls of her golden brown hair are blowing across her forehead and on her uncovered head; her dark eyes are just sparkling with fun and merriment, while her sweet face seems alight with her rare smile which is so wholesome and, I wish I might say, tender, for that best describes it.

I am quite certain that I have never looked at her so closely or discovered so much that pleases. Somehow she seems to me now altogether a different personage and one from whom no need exists why I should hold myself aloof.

For that matter, from the very first she has impressed me as superior in every way to her lowly station and I have found nothing in her manner, appearance and words but what strengthens this feeling. And now, possibly due to her intimate association with Mr. McPherson in their game and her own rare accomplishment of this gentlemanly art, I am aware of an altogether strange and new regard for her and of a sudden, curious sensation that, as I stand there waiting, this sweetly beautiful girl is actually walking straight into my life.

Out of the Rough

I cannot explain it. But the impression, seeming to come upon me from some other source than through my own thoughts, is almost startling in its vividness. It is as if I have just been told this quite absurd idea, not through word of mouth, but by some agency that is understandable to a sense less obvious than that of hearing.

I only know that I am conscious of the impression for a fleeting instant and concerned with it no further at the time. But I daresay that some of the admiration that I cannot deny so charming and excellent a player may appear in my steady look, for she smiles at me pleasantly as she addresses her ball for the putt, and I doff my cap, a bit awkwardly I fear, and wait silently beside Sandy while they halve the hole in a perfect three.

"Forty-five to the turn," calls Mr. McPherson gaily, as I shake hands with both. "Not bad—eh, Sandy? And now for a four to make it an eighty-nine."

Eighty-nine! And this is the man I am to play in less than two weeks!

"Aye, an' how much are ye doun tae th' lassie?" queries Sandy slyly.

"Ah, that is a different matter," replies Mr. McPherson with ready good-nature. "Five and four, isn't it, Jeanie?"

"Oh, but ye hae gien me twa putts that should na count," she responds brightly.

And as I turn to wait for her while she exchanges her putter for a driver, I perceive the caddies glance at each other with curious expressions.

"Miss Jeanie," I tell her as we walk together to the tee, "you are altogether wonderful. I have been watching you from the sixteenth on."

She gives me a quick, amused glance at this. Altogether she seems just bubbling over with joyous spirits; not because of her victory over the affable minister, I am sure; but from sheer enjoyment with the game, the fresh, open air and bright sunshine and something else, it seems to me, lurking just behind the laughter in her dark eyes.

That night I endeavor to reason out the problem Sandy has given me, but for some reason my thoughts will not stay long upon it. Coming back to it again and again I go so far as to deduce that the forcing muscles should not be the guiding muscles; yet, from my conception of the stroke, that conclusion raises such confusing and contradictory ideas that I see no way to clarify it. For surely the hands, under the control of the arm muscles, must do the guiding, and if the power is not given to the stroke by the arms, whence does it come?

Then there recurs to me Sandy's remark that half the village will be on hand to witness my match with

You are altogether wonderful!

the minister. This fills me with momentary misgivings, for I have always been rather shy about playing before people; but not for long. My thoughts insist upon wandering along and, just why I do not know, I set myself to think over all the circumstances that induced Bosworth's letter to me, which only a few hours ago had so filled me with anger and resentment. To my surprise, I am conscious of neither emotion now, and in a little while the whole matter drifts from my mind.

And in its place, there accompanies me into dreamland, the vision of a bright stretch of rolling green, warm sunshine slanting through the trees and in the midst of it all a strong, slender girl walking straight toward me, with dark eyes that shine dazzlingly as they look into mine.

IX

I AWAKE this morning in uncommonly good spirits that seem peculiarly attuned to the brightness and freshness of the early day. When I become aware of it, I ascribe my lightheartedness to a complete absence of the headache which had so oppressed me the morning before. Soon, however, I am dimly aware that it is something apart from my physical well being; that it has more to do with the condition of the mind.

It puzzles me slightly, while I am busy with my razor, although I am too gay at heart to consider the matter seriously. Unconsciously, I am actually humming as I lather my face and get ready the blade. The effect, while perhaps not particularly tuneful, is at least cheery but when I finally find myself at it, I am surprised into sudden silence through its rarity to my morning awakenings of many months past.

Being somewhat prone to analysis, I take my cold tub thoughtfully, and am half finished with my dressing with only a vague inkling of what is behind my unaccountable feeling of gaiety. Then abruptly I sense that my mind this morning is untroubled by some long pressing matter that had been loath of settlement.

Before I quite gather the meaning of that impression, I am acutely conscious that whatever it is, the perturbing question has been settled—definitely and happily settled so far as I am concerned.

Then, suddenly, the truth dawns upon me. It is Angelica!

With the full realization, I face the fact boldly and proceed to probe my feelings in the matter. I discover no uneasiness in mind, although I am well aware that apprehension was the inalienable companion of my earlier regard. I see now too, what my stubborn will heretofore refused to admit, that the whole affair was cloaked with utter hopelessness. But with this tardy recognition there is no despair. In fact I am laughing, quite heartily; for without ambition there can scarcely be defeat. And assuredly I have no longer the least ambition in fair Angelica's regard.

Abruptly my mirth is checked. I am conscious of another emotion that takes quick hold upon me and grows apace. It is a feeling of resentment. I decide that I have been most scurrilously treated. I do not at once recognize the immediate source of this sudden emotion until I recall Bosworth's letter of yesterday. Ah, that is it. My friends have been enjoying a considerable joke at my expense. Perhaps that is the cause also of the sudden transition in the state of my own regard for the fair but fickle lady of the links.

I complete my dressing, without haste, and drag the abominable missive from the place to which I had carelessly consigned it. When I am finished with it and watch the last ash curl and wither in the broad fireplace, I have a new plan built upon the structure of the old and with vastly sounder foundation. My mission, I tell myself, will hardly be that of revenge, but it will be at least one of retaliation.

Once again I take my resolve, but now with far stronger purpose than at any time hitherto: I shall master this game!

I attack Bob's porridge and bacon with the greatest gusto. My spirits are more buoyant than ever. Truly, this morning, I have a double awakening.

I must have come late to my breakfast; for Bob after a very casual "Guid mornin'," has left me to myself. I am glad of that. I am anxious to get back to my problem. . . .

Although the freshness of the morning invites me out, I resolutely return to my room, fill my pipe and seat myself in the chair before the window.

Now then: Sandy made a curious statement whose meaning, he suggested, I might reason out if I thought upon it. He said—the muscles which impart the greater power to the stroke are not so good for guiding it.

[116]

I ponder this for a while, and get nowhere with it. I suspect that it is too advanced for me. Since I have not yet actually hit the ball under Sandy's guidance, I am hardly prepared to analyze the muscular effort given to the full stroke. I, therefore, discard the problem and set my mind to review the fundamentals.

Sandy emphasized the necessity of hitting the ball from a firm balance which must be maintained throughout the stroke.

This is the one thing I had never been able to accomplish.

I am quite agreed in my own mind that I will follow all of Sandy's directions blindly without reference to the faults I had earlier acquired. But I conceive that it might be helpful if I knew just why I had never been able to do this simple thing.

I get up from my chair, lay my pipe aside and grasp a club at random. Taking my stance, I close my eyes and visualize myself on the first tee at Folothru. I want at least, as I have so often desired, a drive of two hundred yards.

With all my strength, I make a vicious swipe. The club shaft tingles in my hands. There is a most ungodly crash and clatter. But I will not be distracted from my purpose.

I hold my position as well as I am able, and open my eyes. My left foot is dragged completely around.

I am standing alone on my bent right leg, and my whole body has swayed backward.

Dropping the club, I take up my pipe and return to the chair. Subconsciously I am aware of voices below, but I pay them no heed.

First: I have finished the stroke with my weight entirely on my right leg, which is utterly incorrect, and my body has moved backward; that is, directly opposite to the movement of the club head.

I see it! I have made a body stroke, and not an arm stroke. All the muscles of my back and shoulders have made that effort. My arms were only dragged around by the strength of my body. Small wonder I could not keep my feet. Firm balance, indeed!

I have taken Sandy's word literally and as gospel, but for the first time I understand clearly the reason that makes his statement on these two points so sound and so impossible of contradiction.

The muscles of the shoulders and the body must not enter into the effort of the stroke, except to turn the body in a pivot and enable hands and club head to complete their arc.

But if the body muscles are not to contribute to the force, whence comes the power to attain the maximum of distance?

It is gratifying to me that I recall instantly my first attempt to cast a fly. When, with the impetus of my body, I swung my arm through stiffly, it availed

[118]

nothing, except a clout in the back of the head as the fly came stumbling along. It was only when my arm, free of any effort contributed to it by my body, moved smoothly forward and, at the exact moment of timing, my wrist flicked forward, that the fly shot straight onward to a far greater distance.

I think then of the wheat threshing. When body and arms swept mightily with the handle, the tail-end, or swingle as Sandy called it, was more apt to catch me a sound thump on elbow or leg than to hit the pile of wheat at all. But as my arms moved without body effort and swung the handle at such speed that carried the swingle in proper line, then the timed flick, again, produced the best of results.

This picture brings a new thought to my mind.

Sandy spoke yesterday, somewhat mysteriously, of an idea of his own that is the very keynote to the stroke's greatest possible efficiency. I have a glimmering—— By Jove! I almost think——

I become abruptly aware that the door of my room is open; that Bob Ferguson is framed there, regarding ruefully myself and the room before him. At his shoulder appears the frightened face of a maid. I rise to my feet in bewilderment, speculating what dire misfortune might have happened below.

"Fegs, laddie," Bob says soberly, with a shake of the head, "are ye fair bent on deemolishin' th' place?"

"Eh?" I ejaculate in surprise.

I follow his glance. On a small table, at its very edge, stands the base, with ragged circumference, of what had been a bowl. A little water still stands in the bottom. On the rug below it are a broad wet spot, a fragment of the bowl and some long stemmed roses. More roses and smaller fragments lead straight away from the spot. My eyes follow the trail of disaster to the farther wall where, waist high, a bit of porcelain is actually imbedded in the plaster.

I glance back. My brassie is lying beside the table, to its right as I am facing it. Something about that relative position strikes me as strange, but I have no time to consider it now.

I look at Ferguson who turns from his glum inspection of the damage to regard me with a somewhat puzzled expression.

"I'm terribly sorry, Bob," I say. "I'm not quite sure just how it happened, but please put it all on my bill, and add to the damage something for the trouble of clearing up."

"Ye need hae na doot I'll put it on th' bill," Bob grumbles, still looking at me with that curious expression. "But ye say ye dinna ken how ye did it?"

"Well you see, Bob, I was thinking out a problem of the stroke that Sandy gave me, and I took a swing with my eyes closed. Then I was so absorbed——"

"Guid losh!" Bob interrupts. " 'Tis th' grand luck

ye nae had yer een open or ye'd bashed a hole in the wa'."

He shakes his head again, and looks down at the rug where the maid is gathering the fragments and the strewn roses.

" 'Tis a pity for th' puir roses, and Jeanie——"

"Do you mean to say—Miss Jeanie picked those —for me?"

Bob looks at me, and for the first time since his entrance, there is a faint twinkle in his dour glance.

"Aye, laddie; an' everra mornin' wi' her ain twa hands."

"Great Caesar, Bob! I'd no idea of that. Will you please thank her for me, and tell her how much I appreciate her kindness?"

"I'm thinkin', th' man ye are, it would be weel to thank her yersel'."

He steps to the door and pauses.

"Kitty," he says, in a very sober voice, "if master Hale still be wantin' his roses and is daft on playin' gowf in th' housie, ye maun fetch up tae him th' coal scuttle. It winna break sae easy."

X

I AM sure that I had been almost upon the point of an important discovery in the stroke when Bob's arrival in my room interrupted my thought. I try to put my mind upon the matter anew, but find it difficult to attain the necessary concentration. Besides, there is the maid busily cleaning up the debris from my unfortunate experiment, with my room yet to put in order.

My eyes fall upon the roses which Kitty is gathering in one hand. Surely I must find Miss Jeanie and render my tardy acknowledgment. I am aware that the thought of her picking these beautiful flowers for me is a very pleasing one.

By Jove! what a wonderful figure she was with her graceful, powerful swing—and then when she walked toward me, as Sandy and I waited beside the green.

Suddenly I recall my vision of this slender, beautiful girl, that accompanied my thoughts last night into dreamland. As instantly I think of my awakening to discover what little place Angelica holds in my regard. I wonder if this, rather than Bosworth's letter, might not have worked the strange happening.

I am a little disturbed by the reflection, but not unpleasantly. . . .

By this time I have found my cap and stuffed pipe and tobacco pouch into my pockets. As I near the door I hear Bob's hearty, rolling laughter, somewhere below, and a lighter, sweeter tone which I recognize instantly as Miss Jeanie's voice. I am glad that I can thank her at once.

Confound the man! What a picture he must have drawn of me to this girl.

I descend rather heavily, for the stairs have a most abrupt pitch. I recall the difficulty I encountered in climbing them the evening of the fish dinner, and the remembrance causes me to laugh aloud. I do not hear its echo in those other voices.

The big room is deserted, save for the tapster busy behind his barrels and kegs at the farther end. I wander outside and around the Inn. There is no one at all in the garden that stretches all the way to the white Manse beyond.

I fill my pipe and stroll slowly into the village. The streets are lined with great trees through which the bright sunlight filters. The air is fresh, but very warm. Distantly I hear the ring of hammer or anvil, a curiously cheering sound. Everything is peacefully quiet.

I stop before the wide open door and dusty window of a jeweler's shop. I see the little old proprietor bent low over his counter, his spectacles far down his nose, peering at some work he holds in his hands. There is a show-case beside him and trinkets on the wall behind. There are also things in the window, but the glass is too grimed and stained to make out just what they are.

I must make some amends for those roses that have gone without even acknowledgment, to say nothing of thanks, these several days.

The little man doesn't even glance up as I enter. It is only when I take my watch from my pocket and shove it beneath his glasses that he gives an impatient gesture, scowls, pushes his spectacles close to his eyes and looks at me.

His eyes brighten quickly.

"Guid mornin', master Hale," he greets me. " 'Tis a recht braw day in th' makin'."

It is strange how quickly one becomes known to these good people who are so invariably courteous.

I ask him if he will look at my watch to see if it needs cleaning. While he is busy over it, I glance in the window, whose contents are visible from the shop side, look at the wall and finally turn to the little show-case. There is a very small wrist-watch in it, with gold chain bracelet. It is quite modern in design, and I am surprised that it should be here. I decide that it is exactly what I want. I ask him to show it to me.

He sets my own watch aside to comply, and I slip
it into my pocket. The wrist-watch is of good Swiss
make. I am surprised at the price; it is less than I
had expected. He tells me that just recently he had
gotten it in "Edinburra."

There is a dainty little case for it, and he puts that
in a small box. As I am leaving, he gestures toward
my pocket and says that my watch is in very good
shape.

I go into the sunlit street and have the feeling that
he is at the door of his shop watching me saunter
along.

I try to recall my interrupted thought of the
morning, but again find it not easy to put my mind
upon it. I decide to postpone the matter, at least
until I go to my afternoon lesson. Since I have made
my purchase, I have become a little self-conscious. I
do not understand why.

I make one or two further stops in the village,
one a little outside, and then set off for a brisk walk
in the hills.

The whole countryside is so calm and serene that
I cannot quite reconcile my slight feeling of restless-
ness. No doubt the walk and the fresh air off the
water will quiet me. I want to be in excellent shape
for Sandy this afternoon. . . .

Miss Jeanie is not visible at the Inn when I return
for luncheon. I do not ask for her. I feel that I should

like to see her first away from these people who are
so uniformly kind but who, in some unaccountable
manner, seem to know exactly what one is doing; and
I daresay if I had come upon her I should hardly
have offered my little token of appreciation there.

My appetite, from my walk, is excellent, and I
relish the good things Bob has had prepared for me.
My spirits again are buoyant as I bound up to my
room. Nothing bothers me in the least. I can give my
whole mind to the work of the afternoon.

My roses are there, in a fresh bowl. It is not on
the table, however, but placed, perhaps for greater
security, on the mantel. I find it strange that I should
have looked for them the first thing, while heretofore
I had scarcely given them a thought, although, to be
sure, I was always aware of their presence. . . .

Sandy is waiting for me, standing before the door
of his little shop and puffing his pipe serenely. There
is something wholesomely solid in his appearance.

"Hae ye thought oot th' leetle problem, Bob,"
he greets me, "that I hae gie' ye yestere'en?" The
question is sober enough, but there is a curious
twinkle in his eyes.

"I almost had it, Sandy," I say, a little excitedly,
"when——"

"When ye hae taen that braw swipe at Bob's mug
of roses?"

Now how in Heaven's name could he have heard of
[126]

that mishap so speedily! It is an unending mystery to me in what manner news travels so swiftly among these people when they appear to move about hardly at all.

Sandy's laugh is so hearty that I have, perforce, to join in it.

"But seriously, Sandy, I learned much from that."

"I dinna doot it, laddie, an' muckle mair ye'll l'arn when ye hae Bob's bill o' damages."

"I found out," I persist, in spite of Sandy's chuckling, "just exactly why you cannot put any effort of back or shoulders into the stroke. If you do, it swings you around off your feet and not only draws the club head across the ball but also kills all the force you want to give to the impact. You have told me all these things, but now I see them for the first time clearly."

"It was perhaps nae sic a bad experiment after a'."

Sandy draws the back of his hand across his eyes, stuffs a finger into his pipe and puts the pipe into his pocket.

"But there is one thing I wish you would explain to me, Sandy—since you know what happened. The bowl was on a table at a level with my hips. The table was directly behind me when I made the swing. However did I hit it? And I must have hit it very squarely, because a bit of the bowl went straight back and stuck in the wall."

"Ye was——" Sandy interrupted himself to let out another roar of laughter; but he sobered quickly —— "Ye was reachin' for th' ba', Bobbie. An' I was comin' tae that. Ye maun hae th' ba' within easy distance of th' club head as ye staund tae it. If ye reach fer it, ye'll swing around an' that's nae a pivot at a'."

"Then that was why I finished so low? And I must have hit the bowl on the finish, for the table was behind me."

"Aye, Bob; awa below yer shouther, when ye maun finish above it. But ye can mak that a' recht in th' backswing."

Sandy reaches into the doorway and brings out the driver he has had me use before. He hands it to me, and I carefully take the grip as he has described it; with my left thumb straight down the shaft on the side opposite the club face, which brings my knuckles uppermost, and with my right hand slightly over the shaft. The little finger of that hand overlaps the forefinger of my left; the palm is pressed against the left thumb, and the club is held between right thumb and the second joint of the forefinger.

"Guid, Bobbie. Now waggle it. Verra guid. Ye see th' twa wrists bend ane wi' tither an' nae separate like twa hinges apairt. Noo tak yer stance, laddie."

[128]

Out of the Rough

I place my feet on a line with the prospective flight of the ball and fairly close together. Then I allow my hands, and consequently my shoulders, to drop and let the club head rest directly opposite my left heel. I try to stand easily and not tense.

"Verra guid," Sandy approves again, "but there are ane or twa things mair tae it. Dinna bend mair, but let th' end of th' club touch th' woo' of yer pants. Sae. That brings th' club head, an' th' ba', closer tae ye. It also drops yer recht shouther a wee bit, which will start it gaun in th' proper direction. Noo, Bobbie, turn yer left foot in, almost straight tae th' ba'. That will help ye tae hold yer balance when ye finish th' stroke. Ane thing mair. Stick oot th' tail of yer spine, laddie. It'll tak th' weight off yer taes."

When I comply with the latter injunction, I find that my back, instead of bowing outward, is bent slightly inward, and I seem to stand more firmly. I had never thought of that before.

"Noo, slow; tak yer backswing."

Keeping my eyes steadily on the spot where the club head rested, I bend my left knee in, toward my straight right leg, and continuing the motion it gives to my shoulders, carry my hands back and upward as far as my straight left arm will allow. It seems to me that I have done it correctly.

"Hauld it recht there," Sandy tells me. " 'Tis nae sae bad, an' nae sae guid. But ye maun hae th' backswing a' recht if ye are tae mak th' stroke proper. Turn yer head an' leuk where th' club head is."

I do so and observe that shaft and club head are slightly below my right shoulder.

"What did I do wrong, Sandy?"

"Fer ane thing ye carried yer hands tae far tae th' recht an' back of ye. Fer anither, ye let yer left wrist bend yer fist in, when ye maun keep it straight or bent a wee bit in tither direction."

With my hands still up, Sandy carries them a little forward and straightens my left wrist. In this position, shaft and club head are more nearly over my body.

"Put it doun, Bobbie, an' dae it again, and this time keep yer recht elbow tae yer side. That wull put yer han's in th' proper place at th' top of th' swing."

I do it very slowly and very carefully. Sandy nods his head.

"Can ye remember a' that, Bobbie?"

"I'll never forget it," I tell him seriously.

"Then ye'll never gang far wrang. Maist everrabody'll dae it when they're told, but in th' heat of th' stroke they forget. Th' backswing is maist important. If ye dinna hae a fair start, ye'll hae a puir finish. Dinna forget that, laddie. An' yer club maun start from half way betwixt yer head an' yer recht shouther.

"Noo, tae gang on wi' what I set oot tae explain. Tak yer stance ance mair."

As I do so, Sandy sticks a little sliver of wood in the ground against the center of the club face.

"That's yer ba'," he explains.

He then draws in the sand a straight line directly back from the direction the ball should take and parallel to the line of my feet. He draws another line from toe to toe and extends it to match the first in length.

"Noo, remember, Bobbie, that when yer club head comes doun it maun approach th' ba' frae th' line of yer feet, an' when it hits th' ba' it maun gang oot beyond tither line."

"I remember, Sandy. From the inside out and through."

I take my backswing slowly, making sure that my left wrist bends inward, that is, to carry the hand outward from my body, and that my hands are not brought around too far to my right and back of me. I am careful too that my shoulders pivot naturally with the upward swing of my arms and without conscious effort of their muscles. My left shoulder presses against my chin; my right shoulder is above it.

"Guid; noo doun an' through."

My left knee, bent inward toward my right on the upswing, starts back to its straight position. At the same time, my left thumb presses the shaft, while, simultaneously, the back of my left arm and my right forearm start the downward motion. I am not in the least hurried. I accelerate this motion, and as hands and club head get low, I push my right hand down and outward. My right shoulder follows and goes ahead of my left; my weight shifts forward. The club head swings above my body, and considerably to my own astonishment, my left leg is straight and I am still firmly on my feet. I am sure that never before have I made such a swing.

"Noo ye see, Bobbie, that when yer backswing is a' recht an' proper an' ye hae nae reached fer yer ba', ye can keep yer feet weel under ye. Leuk at yer club th' noo."

I raise my head and see that my hands have finished high, and that the club extends backward between my head and left shoulder, just the reverse of the top position of my back swing.

Sandy has me repeat the performance a dozen times; and each time it seems to me that my motions are smoother, more assured and more certain. He then takes the driver from me.

"That," he tells me, "is what I want tae mak clear. If everra time ye tak yer backswing and yer forward swing exactly like that, mak yer recht shouther gang doun an' through an' let yer weight gang wi' yer pivot tae yer straight left leg, ye can gie a' yer strength to yer arms and wrists an' never leave yer twa feet.

"There's mair tae it, afore ye'll hae th' stroke a' proper. But sae far, I'm verra satisfied. Th' rest is yer ain business."

"What do you mean, Sandy?" I ask, a little perplexed.

" 'Tis this, laddie. I hae shown ye th' stroke an' how tae dae it. If ye mind it a' th' time an' everra time, ye can mak a gowfer. If ye dinna mind it an' gang on yer ain, ye canna, an' th' deil himsel' could nae help ye."

"But, Sandy, that is exactly what I intend to do, and nothing else."

Sandy sets the driver away, pulls his pipe from his pocket and strikes a match above it.

"That's a' fer th' day, Bobbie."

He turns and enters his shop.

XI

I THINK of what Sandy has said as I fill my pipe and walk slowly down the little hill. Having been one of the worst of duffers who have tried seriously to play the game, I appreciate fully the truth of his remark.

It is of course perfectly obvious that while knowledge of how to make the stroke properly is all important, unless I follow his instructions all the time and do not once deviate from them, I can in no way help myself.

I am glad that he put it that way, for it will stick in my mind. I shall make no more experiments of my own: although I can scarcely regret the one of the morning since it made clear to me the reason underlying one of Sandy's basic points.

It seems to me now that the cardinal principle of all is not to put body effort into the swing. The arms are to do all the work; give all the impetus and force to the stroke. Let the body pivot to give the hands the greater arc they must have to supply the necessary speed and power to the club head. But there must be no conscious body effort.

Out of the Rough

This fact is very clear before me. I comprehend it fully and with far more clarity than when Sandy first told me of it some days ago. Nevertheless, I realize the difficulties that lie before me if I am always to hold to this maxim.

First I must learn to control my muscles so that my arms will act by themselves, apart from whatever impulse may be given them by the pivoting body. I am wondering in what manner I can best set about this when I recall my lesson in fly casting. To be sure, that expresses it exactly. When I finally acquired something of the knack, I remember that, no matter if my body swayed, my right arm worked quite independently, going out as if of its own volition, with the flick of the wrist at the right moment, and with no relation whatsoever to body movement or effort.

I am thinking what a really extraordinary instructor is Sandy Macgregor, when I am startled from my deep meditation.

"Guid evenin', master Hale!"

I know the voice even before I glance up—there is scarcely another like it that I have ever heard. I have come down the hill and am in the little lane, close to the corner. Miss Jeanie, who apparently has just stepped from Grannie Robertson's cottage, is almost beside me.

"Oh, Miss Jeanie," I exclaim, "I am so glad to see you!"

Possibly I have spoken too impulsively. Having looked for her all day, and then to come upon her so abruptly has caught me unawares.

Color is rich in her cheeks as she gives me a quick look which seems to me a little puzzled. Then she laughs very heartily, in her sweet, low voice that is so vibrant in tone. She cocks her head a bit to one side; her brown eyes are dancing.

"Are ye always sae bent on gowf, master Hale, that ye maun play it in th' housie?"

I laugh with her. We walk along together.

"But I am very glad it happened," I tell her. "Otherwise I might never have known of my long debt to you: I am so stupidly absent-minded." I take the little package from my pocket. "Miss Jeanie, I am going to ask a great favor of you. I want you to relieve me from embarrassment."

She takes it from me, almost mechanically, and holds it in the slender fingers of both hands. I glance at her and observe that the color has left her cheeks; her eyes have grown very dark, and I think there is a little moisture in them.

"For me!" she breathes in a tone so low it is hardly audible. "I do not think that I should take it."

"If you will be so kind," I hasten to assure her. "You see, I don't want you to think me ungrateful. I have really appreciated those beautiful roses, and

[136]

every day they were so fresh. But only this morning I learned that I was indebted to you."

"But that was nothing," she says slowly. She continues to look at me so soberly and with such curious expression that I can only think she is making more of this slight gift than she should. A poor girl, no doubt she is not used to them. "The garden is full of roses," she adds, "and I always think it a pity others should not enjoy them. Really you should not do this."

"No?" I say, and try to laugh a little. My feeling of slight embarrassment is quite unaccountable. "I insist that it is a personal debt. Besides, I assure you there is no one in the world to whom I would rather give a little token of this sort. So you see, as you say, it is nothing."

She still regards me seriously and, I think, somewhat searchingly.

"In some ways, Mr. Hale, you are a very strange man. I should say that most people, even your close acquaintances, do not really know you at all. I have never met anyone quite like you, but I think I understand you. Now, for example, unless by accident one would scarcely imagine that almost daily you have visited the poorest people in the village and helped them."

Now I am quite embarrassed.

"But, you see, Miss Jeanie, I have never before

been among people who, of all sorts, are so genuinely friendly to a stranger."

We had stopped by the hedgerow in the lane.

She shakes her head slowly, but is smiling a little. She glances down at the package in her hands. I had not before observed how long her lashes are. She is extremely lovely.

"May I look at it?" she asks, without raising her eyes.

"Why, surely. It is yours."

She unties the string and slips off the paper, but does not crumple it. She lifts out the wrist-watch with a little exclamation.

"Oh, this is too beautiful! Is it really meant for me?"

She glances quickly at me, and her eyes are very bright and glowing.

"For no one else!"

Slowly she replaces the watch and neatly ties the package. We start on. She is sober again, and appears thoughtful.

"I thank you very much," she says, in her low tone. And after a little while: "I really do not know what I should do. I want to keep it. May—may I ask my father?"

"Oh, by all means. But of course you will keep it. There is no reason in the world why you should not."

"I do not know."

[138]

"But I am only too happy if it gives you any pleasure."

"It does—very much."

We approach the spot where the path branches off from the Inn to lead beyond.

"Oh, Miss Jeanie," I say, "I wonder, after Sandy has taught me further, if you would be willing to play a round with us. There are so many things I want to ask."

"I should like to. I hope we may . . . I leave you here; I must go on. . . . Good night," she says a little hurriedly. She is not smiling at all.

My pipe has gone out. As I stop to relight it I watch her swinging stride as she goes around the Inn and from my sight. Something troubles me that I do not quite understand.

I daresay I am rather absent-minded as I climb to my room and start to change from my golfing clothes for dinner. I am a bit elated over my progress with Sandy, and altogether I have a peculiarly comforting glow of good feeling.

I plunge my hands into the cold water of the basin and splash my face. Suddenly I stop in the midst of my ablutions. The solution of my recent perplexity has abruptly come to me.

From the instant I had given the package to Miss Jeanie she had ceased to speak in the dialect of the

Scottish people! Her words were as purely English as could possibly be. Now this is strange. . . .

I decide that I will speak to no one, not even Bob Ferguson, of my discovery. I shall see her of course in the morning, and will talk further with her.

XII

THE morning passes rather swiftly. I am looking forward with keen zest to my meeting with Sandy in the afternoon. Again and again I have reviewed in my mind the principles he has laid down for me to follow. The things to do and those to be avoided are so clearly impressed upon me that I am confident I shall make no mistake. I am anxious to put myself to the test.

Then, too, perhaps on my way back I shall meet Miss Jeanie. She seems to go quite regularly to Grannie Robertson's, which is on my way to and from Sandy's. My curiosity is greatly aroused. Of course her manner of speech, or rather change of speech, may be quite ordinary; but I feel that there is something about her that I have not fully understood. Somehow I am not satisfied that she fits exactly into her environment. . . . She is exquisitely dainty—so wholesome, so transparent in character one can perceive that she is wholly good and generous hearted.

I have not seen her all morning.

After luncheon and a slow pipe, I set out briskly.

Sandy hands me the driver, without greeting. He appears more than usually sober and thoughtful.

"Ye'll tak your swing th' noo," he says, and his voice sounds a little gruff.

While I take my stance and get the feel of the club, I swiftly review the many different parts of the stroke. Slowly I raise my hands, careful, with my left wrist properly bent, that they do not go too far around my body. I bring them down with increasing speed and push my right shoulder under and forward. The club head comes nicely above my head, and I have been unaware of any inclination to leave my feet. I am sure that my weight shifted at the right moment to my left leg which now is straight.

"Nae sae bad," Sandy rumbles. "Dae it ane time mair."

I repeat the stroke, giving a little more force to my arms.

"Ane time mair."

A dozen times I make the swing, and it seems to me that I am actually getting a smooth rhythm from start to finish.

Sandy turns from me to step inside his shop. He is out in a moment with a landing net in which are a number of golf balls. Without a word, he sets out, and I follow.

We cross the meadow behind the cottage and come to the nearby links which appear to be deserted.

Sandy goes on to the third tee, but faces away from its own fairway toward that of the fifth which parallels the third in the reverse direction and is somewhat more level. He tees a ball, steps back to me and nods.

Up to that very moment I have been calm and confident; but now I come up to my stance with a sense of that familiar misgiving which had accompanied me every time I started to play. I am conscious that my stroke is hurried. The ball goes out, not far, and with a very bad slice. I am dismayed.

"Sandy," I groan, "let me stop now to ask you something."

"Weel, laddie?"

"For God's sake, tell me what I must do to keep my body out of it!"

"In the first place ye were braced to drive a mallet agee a spike. A gowf ba' is a wee thing, nae muckle mair than a thistle. A verra sma' tap wi' th' club head will send it as far as ye can wish. There's nae weight tae it ava. Ye're feart of it, man.

"Noo—ye maun start your doun swing wi' a sma' movement of your left knee and pullin' doun wi' your hands. Ye maun be verra careful that your shouthers dinna turn wi' your knee and start ahead of your han's. Ye maun be sure everra time that your han's *start first* an' th' turning of your shouther *follows behind* your han's an' helps tae push them through."

[143]

I repeat for myself:

"Be sure that your shoulders do not turn with the movement of your left knee. Feel that your hands are starting first, and that the body pivot follows them down."

Sandy tees another ball.

"This time, Robert, dinna lift your left heel ava. Keep baith feet firm tae th' grun when your knee bends in, an' hae confidence in th' strength of your arms. Loosen up your body, man. Nae be sae tense."

Summoning all my control of will, I do exactly as he directs, and in addition make the stroke with very little effort at all.

To my astonishment, the ball goes straight out and as far as ever I have driven.

"But, Sandy," I cry, "I only tapped it!"

"Sae I have tauld ye, mony's th' time," Sandy says, very dryly.

"But it's the simplest thing in the world!"

"Aye, an' that's th' gowf stroke. Th' mair ye put tae it, the less ye dae. A lit'le tap, wi' th' club head gaun in th' proper direction is a'."

I drive a half dozen balls, one after the other. Every one goes out fairly straight, without the sign of a slice, and as I gain confidence and raise my left heel a little, lengthening my back swing, the distance is increased. I have been scarcely aware of any particular muscular effort. I am amazed and delighted.

[144]

"Sandy, how can I remember and do it again?"

"Ye can dae it everra time, Robert, if ye will keep what I told ye in min'. Rest a bit th' noo."

Sandy takes the driver from me and tees a ball for himself. I watch with all eyes.

His great hands close lightly around the grip. He takes his stance with a glance down the fairway. His backswing is so slow, so deliberate that I think it is only a practice swing. Then the club head starts down.

There is a sharp "crack." The ball shoots out like a rifle bullet, straight as an arrow, low. Away out it begins to climb; then curves downward with a slight pull to the left and settles to run and stop a hundred yards beyond my best effort.

Sandy is standing erect, firmly on both feet, leaning slightly forward with his right shoulder ahead. There is a little twinkle in his gray eyes as he observes my look of awe.

"As I hae tauld ye, Robert, 'tis a wee tap that daes it."

"But it seemed to me a mighty stroke, Sandy. Look at the distance you got!"

"That's whaur ye're wrang. Th' main thing, Robert, is that I can mak' th' club head come up tae th' ba' in th' proper line, hit it square in th' center an' stay recht wi' it till it gangs awa. I mak it gang through an' oot an' I dinna pull it in till it haes done its work. That's th' secret of a guid stroke. Hit th' ba' fair an' square an' keep th' head behind it till it's expanded an' gone awa. An' ye canna dae that unless ye shove th' club head oot wi' th' recht shouther gaun under an' ahead.

"Sin' I can dae that everra time, I gie strength tae my forearms, my wrists an' my han's, tae throw th' club head doun an' through, an' I gie th' maist of my strength just when I hit th' ba', but nane tae my shouthers or my body."

"Good Lord, Sandy, what wouldn't I give to be able to make a drive like that!"

"Ye can dae it, Robert, when ye learn tae hit th' ba' proper everra time, but dinna try tae dae it th' noo, or ye'll spoil th' guid ye already hae."

Sandy passes me the driver and tees a ball. I expect, unconsciously, I am thinking of his own mighty drive, for my first attempt is a miserable failure. I know my hands went up in the right direction, and came down without effort of my body, and that my right shoulder followed through and out. But the club head hit the ground six inches short of the ball and barely got it away at all. I look at Sandy in dismay.

"Ye whupped it like a lash, man. Your han's went up an' doun so fast that they started doun, along wi' your recht shouther, afore ever th' club head stopped gaun on th' upswing. Wi' your shouther doun too soon an' your arm straight, when the club head came along it couldna help but hit th' grun. Count your stroke, Robert. Slow—a-n-e-e—on th' upswing; noo, doun, t-t-wa!"

I count slowly to myself: o-n-e-e, as my hands go up: a little pause, and—t-two-o-o! as they come down and through. I repeat it and feel that I am getting some sort of rhythm and a sense of just when to exert greater strength in my wrists; that is, at the moment of impact.

My next drive is more successful. I drive four more balls, in slow succession, and all are beyond the longest of my first half dozen. I am very much encouraged and eager to continue.

"That's a', Robert. We'll gang pick them up."

I must look my disappointment.

"Ye hae haed twalve drives. Wi' a mashie or an iron for th' short holes, ye'll nae hae mair than fifteen drives in a full round of th' links; an' ye'll hae five minutes or mair between them. If ye dae muckle mair th' noo, ye'll forget th' maist important pairts of th' stroke, an' your bad habits will come back tae ye."

I take one more practice swing, with the slow count. Almost, almost I think I have it. I hope only that it will stay with me. It is nearly a silent prayer.

Sandy says not a word as we go hither and yon to pick up my scattered drives. He has fallen into his reserve again, and altogether seems cool and aloof. Today he has addressed me only as "Robert," which is significant of his feeling. Naturally I have not the least suspicion why. I presume he is subject to moods —like Bob Ferguson, and one or two others I have observed.

He stops, however, when we come to his own ball.

"Aboot twa hunner an' fifty; an' your last was fair close tae twa hunner an' verra guid. I wouldna see it better th' noo. If there's ane thing that'll put a gowfer off his stroke it is tae try tae outbeat a powerfu' driver. Remember that weel, Robert.

"When ye came tae mak your drive followin' mine ain, ye were sae bent on gettin' tae th' ba' that ye thought of naithing else. Remember weel that your han's dinna gang straight tae th' ba'. They dinna cut across. They maun gang *down* on a curve, at the end of your straight left arm, then up tae th' ba' an' through."

XIII

WE are both silent as we pace across the links and the little meadow toward Sandy's cottage; but with each, it is from a different cause. Sandy is dour; either troubled about something or in gloomy spell. On the contrary, I am secretly elated at my progress, but I am deep in thought over his last remark.

As I now recall my every attempt to make a long drive—even my most recent endeavor immediately following Sandy's magnificent ball—I remember a sense of trying to get to the ball with the utmost speed possible. With his explanation, I can see that in so doing I neglected to take account of the full path of the proper swing.

The hands must first go downward, then forward to the ball and through, in the arc prescribed by the straight left arm. I shall keep that in mind.

Just now, however, I am happy over the assurance that I can really and truly hit the ball in the right way—at last. I glance up at Sandy to see if his expression gives any indication of satisfaction at the promise I am showing.

He does not even look at me. His face is set in sober lines.

He stops before his cottage and turns to gaze across the lowlands.

"There's a thuck fog driftin' in," he rumbles, as if to himself. "Nae doot we'll hae a wet necht. . . . Guid necht, Robert." He turns and leaves me.

I had not before noticed that in place of the bright sunshine of late afternoon, the sky is obscured and the whole landscape is dull, with a thick bank toward the water. But I make nothing of that; my spirits are too buoyant. Besides, we have had fogs before, but it has always been bright and cheerful in the morning.

I have much to engage my thoughts, yet I am not so absent-minded as on the preceding afternoon. As I walk slowly down the little hill, I cannot refrain from frequent glances toward Grannie Robertson's little white house. Yesterday Miss Jeanie surprised me by her sudden appearance; I am not to be caught unawares today.

I find myself anxiously anticipating the sight of her slender, graceful figure, her brightly smiling face. To be sure, I want to learn if her father has raised any objections to my slight gift; although, for the life of me, I cannot see why he should. Furthermore, I am tremendously curious to know more of this strange girl who can speak English more correctly

than I, but, outside of this one instance, has allowed
me to suppose she knew nothing save this rather out-
landish dialect of the people.

Not of course that it made her appear less attractive; far from that. Still that unconscious exposition
of greater knowledge has aroused both my curiosity
and interest.

I am in the lane now, opposite the door in the cottage; but there is no movement there. I pause to
apply a match to my already glowing tobacco;
then reluctantly go slowly on. I am quite disappointed.

It is almost like dusk as I approach the Inn, and
distinctly cooler. The fog is drifting through the
trees in the village.

I stop on the porch to finish my pipe and watch
the thickening gray blanket settle in. I stay there
several minutes. . . . Miss Jeanie doesn't appear at
all.

I wonder why the mere matter of a fog should so
dampen the naturally gay spirits of these people.
While at my dinner, Bob scarcely speaks to me at all,
and then only in cool monosyllables, without his usual
joviality.

When he brings me my coffee, I venture to ask him
a question; but his reply gives me no degree of satisfaction. . . . There is a noisy little group at the
tap. Somehow their laughing voices produce in me

a feeling of annoyance. I go to my room as soon as I am finished.

Kitty has laid a fire on the stone hearth, and some-one—probably she—has lighted it just before I came up. Ordinarily the blaze would be bright and cheer-ful. Tonight it seems only to emphasize the presence of the enveloping fog. It is drifting through my partly opened casement. I cross to it.

There is a light in the Manse. I see it as a faint, blurred spot of radiance. Confound this fog!

I leave the window, and settling in my most com-fortable chair, light my pipe. I soon set it aside and pace a bit. . . . I am peculiarly restless. Presently I take up my note book and attempt to jot down my impressions from the afternoon's lesson; but for some reason I find it very difficult to apply my mind to the task with the necessary concentration. I lay the book aside.

I wonder if a stroll through the village will lighten my spirits. I refill my pipe and step to the window to have another look at the weather. I can barely see the light in the Manse at all. The fog filters past me through the casement. It is unutterably dreary and depressing. I daresay I am quite as glum as Sandy or Bob.

I decide against the walk. I stand and glance around the room. Away from the fire, the white-washed walls seem particularly barren. I turn to gaze

[152]

into the flames, with an arm on the mantel, and my thoughts flit from one subject to another, and always return to their starting point.

Bob has told me, in reply to my question at dinner, that Miss Jeanie left Elie on an early morning train. She has gone, he says, to visit friends or relatives in Edinburra. He does not know how long she may be away—possibly a week, perhaps a "fortnecht."

*　　*　　*

The next day drags interminably. There is a fog, but it is my impression that the sun shone through, for a while at least. I am not sure. . . .

I go to Sandy's at the usual hour. Sandy is not there. A gray haired, thin little wisp of a man is standing before the shop door, in a coat that is considerably too large for him. Beneath the peak of an over-sized cap, his face is sharp and ferret-like. He has the driver in one hand; the pockets of his coat are bulged with some weight, causing the garment to hang from his thin shoulders in ludicrous fashion.

"Sandy has gaen feshin'," he greets me. "He tauld me tae tell ye tae drive nae mair than twanty ba's, an' that ye could gie me a shillin'."

I do not find myself especially disappointed. In fact, I have not looked forward to the day's lesson with any particular zest. I expect I have been here so long that the climate has begun to affect me.

[153]

"All right," I tell him. "Will you get the balls?"
He smiles shrewdly.

"I hae them; in ma pocket."

"What is your name?" I ask him, disinterestedly, as we cross the wet meadow.

"They ca' me Tammie," he says. "I hae caddied for twanty year, and I hae seen some grand gowfers in ma time. I'm tae carry yer bag when ye come tae play th' minister."

Somehow I have forgotten all about that impending match, and am not in the least conscious of the nervous feeling of anticipation and inferiority with which I have earlier regarded it.

"Sandy has tauld me I cud safely lay a shillin' or twa on ye, master Hale." He eyes me shrewdly.

I shrug my shoulders.

"I think you'd better not, Tammie. Sandy has more confidence than I."

"I like th' way ye say that, an' I'm thinkin' Sandy canna be sae far wrang. A cauld gowfer is a hard ane tae beat."

Tammie's expression aroused me in a measure from my abstraction. A cold golfer! That had not been exactly my reputation at Folothru.

I approach the tee from which I am to drive, with some degree at least of my former resolution, but at the same time with a fair share of indifference. I take, deliberately, a half dozen practice swings which I am aware Tammie watches critically, although he makes no comment.

At my nod, he tees a ball. I swing at it with none of my customary fervor. To my mild surprise, I get away an astonishingly good drive, straight on the course and somewhat beyond my best effort of yesterday.

"Nae; Sandy wudna be wrang," Tammie mutters. "I'll mak' it a pund, gien th' chance."

I smile a little at this, a bit ruefully.

"That might be all right, Tammie, if I could do that every time; but I assure you I cannot."

"An' why not?" Tammie says heatedly. "Ye hae gaen an' done it th' noo. It's in ye. Ye're ta' an' limber; Sandy has showed ye th' trick of it. Th' rest is a wee matter o' tamperramen', an' ye hae that a' recht too."

*　　　*　　　*

In my lonely room, after dinner, I think over my work of the afternoon and wonder why I am not more elated. I had not really missed one drive, and not once had I sliced. I mildly speculate, too, if after all Tammie has not given me one of the most useful tips—on the matter of temperament.

Throughout the performance, I was aware of a feeling of indifference toward it all, while at home, and even with Sandy, I have been keyed up to the execution of the shot.

No doubt, once the stroke is mastered, therein lies the key to success. But, as a matter of fact, today, and especially this evening, it has occurred to me that I might be taking this question of golf too seriously. There are my affairs at home, for instance.

There was a letter from Bosworth in the morning mail. To be sure, I barely scanned it before I tossed it into the grate; but I recollect he made some mention of market conditions. Bosworth is a broker and at times has handled some of my rare investments. Possibly I have planned too long a stay here. . . . Of course I can remedy that at any time. I think I shall write to the steamship people in London tomorrow to learn what they have for an earlier sailing. . . .

The night is clear, but a little chilly. There doesn't seem to be the usual vigor in the air.

It is very strange. Up until this last fog, I had thought Ferguson the most genial of men. Today he has scarcely spoken to me.

My roses—I have put them back on the table— are becoming faded. Kitty has clipped the stems, as I asked her to do. She was about to throw them out and get me fresh ones, but I bade her not to.

XIV

I SLEEP badly throughout the night. At the first, I tossed for hours and thought I should not get to sleep at all. I awake early, and a bit out of sorts with things. While I am dressing I decide that I shall go out for the day. I do not in the least care to talk with people, and I have the desire to inquire a little further into my own state of mind.

So far as Sandy is concerned, he played me a trick yesterday, and I shall return it in kind. Besides, I'm not so keen on the lesson today. I suspect I have overdone it a trifle. And of course any game, even golf, has its proper place, not of supreme importance, in human relations.

The cook does me up a snack for lunch; I see that my pouch is well filled, pick up a heavy walking stick and start forth.

Bob Ferguson intercepts me at the door. He asks if I shall return in time for my afternoon lesson. I reply noncommittally and very shortly. He has been decidedly surly toward me for the past two days, and, fog or no fog, I shall not pass it unnoticed.

OUT OF THE ROUGH

The day is clear, and the breeze carries a slight tang of the salt water. I walk aimlessly, and for the most part skirt the edge of the lowlands; but they seem endlessly dreary and after a while I go up into the short hills.

I eat my solitary lunch beside a rushing brook. Afterward I stretch on the bank and smoke my pipe in the sun. . . . My thoughts only irritate me and lead me nowhere. I am vaguely oppressed by a sense of being alone. Rather strangely too, for I have never sought close companionship. My experience, with man or woman, has been that thoroughly sympathetic friendship is very rare indeed. In fact, I can truthfully say that I have never enjoyed one. My preference has been for books, my own affairs and my own meditation. Casual acquaintances are all right, if they do not presume too far, for man is gregarious; but most people if one comes to know them too well are inexpressible bores entirely engrossed in their own selfish interests.

When my pipe is finished, I spring abruptly to my feet and walk rapidly and steadily for two hours and more.

I return to the Inn late in the afternoon. I sense the bodily refreshment of fatigue, but my mind is no more at peace than when I started. Throughout the day, a vague suspicion has assailed me that somewhere I have been at fault or have missed doing something. I cannot place it. It both annoys and distresses me, partly, I expect, because of its elusiveness.

I feel, too, that I have been disregarded, pushed aside from an atmosphere that I had counted one wholly of genial warmth. To be sure, I should have become callous to such sensation at home. But here, it was all so different from the beginning—from that blithely sung couplet on my awakening the very first day. And I had thrown myself into the environment of cordial friendliness so whole heartedly, perhaps so inanely. Now in reaction I have become soured and glum. Nothing pleases me.

It's probably that damnable fog! I decide that if I do not have a care I shall return truly a dour Scot.

I complete my bath and change and set myself to write that letter of inquiry to the steamship company. I am half finished with it, when there is a light knock at my door.

I cross the room without haste and open. It is the maid, Kitty. She informs me that Mr. McPherson has called in the morning, and again after luncheon, with the request that I dine this evening at the Manse.

My first impulse is to make excuses; then in time I conquer my selfish churlishness. Mr. McPherson, so often as I have seen him, has shown the soul of good fellowship toward me. And I have not yet met his wife who has been confined to her home by some slight indisposition.

I give Kitty a bit of silver and ask her if she will go over to the Manse, convey my respects and say that I shall be happy to join them at the hour they have suggested.

I lay aside my letter, unfinished.

*   *   *

When I step across the threshold of the Manse I enter an atmosphere of unaffected warmth and cultured friendliness. It is almost as if I am being greeted by the sympathetic figures of my solitary meditation. Mr. McPherson carries his joviality within his home, but its out-of-doors gusto is tempered to the milder tone of the charming lady who is his wife.

Even Mrs. McPherson welcomes me as a friend who already is known and understood. It sets me immediately at my ease and dispels much of my ill feeling of the past days, if not its half suspected cause. She reminds me strongly of someone I have known, but I do not place the resemblance.

The dinner is a simple, wholesome and altogether jolly affair, aided by frequent potions of the excellent ale. Following our coffee, Mr. McPherson pours a generous share of rare Scotch. I have never before tasted its like.

[160]

Out of the Rough

My hosts are so merry, in their subdued way, that I thaw out completely and entertain them with trivial incidents of my college days and later life at home. To their unrestrained amusement, I recount the genesis of my pilgrimage overseas, ascribing as its cause, what might have been true in the beginning and certainly is now, a motive of revenge against my long scoffing club fellows.

"Excellent! Excellent!" applauds the jovial minister, when he has conquered his laughter. "A most cleverly conceived plan that merits and no doubt will win success. Ah—tell me, Robert; are you getting from Sandy all that you hoped for? He is well known for his sparse words and noncommunicativeness."

"Far more than I had expected," I reply enthusiastically. "There is only one drawback in his instruction; and that is really not his fault—rather it is my own."

"And what is that?"

"I am never sure that I understand fully the meaning of his words, and I am anxious not to miss the least shade."

They both laugh heartily at this, in which I find myself joining, although undoubtedly it is somewhat at my expense. Then Mr. McPherson confirms my earlier thought in that matter.

"There is one thing about it, Robert; if you give so much attention to his words, when you finally have

[161]

their import, you are bound to remember the point, which is far better than to let any teaching enter one ear and leave at once by the other."

"But I want to make rapid progress, and I am sure I should get on much faster if there was only someone with me who could explain on the spot the full sense of his meaning."

"That can be easily remedied," says Mr. McPherson, still chuckling, "if we can persuade Jeanie to bear a hand. In these latter days at least, she is Sandy's most capable pupil."

"But Miss Jeanie has gone away," I blurt out, "and no one seems to know when she will return—even," I finish lamely, "if she would be so kind."

"Ahem," says the minister, instantly sober.

He glances at his wife who replies to what I gather is an unspoken question, by her sweet, kindly smile.

"Er—Robert," he begins again. I am at a loss to understand the abrupt seriousness of his tone and manner, and with a sense of imminent confusion sip deeply of my Scotch. "We feel," he goes on, "that even in this short time, we have come to know you as a thoroughly upright young man with the best and most honorable intentions.

"We know of the good you have done with a modesty and secretiveness that commend you. We know your generosity of heart. But you are now in a country whose customs and manners are quite different

[162]

from what I understand to be the pliable and lightly regarded conventions of your own land.

"In Scotland, now, the accepted customs are rigorously and severely upheld. Among our people, the conventions are transgressed only with disaster."

He pauses to sip from his glass.

To what all this is a prelude I cannot possibly conjecture; but, inspired by his words and manner, I have a sudden feeling of guilt, a sense of wrong-doing for which I am to be brought to account. My face feels fiery hot; the room is suddenly close and uncomfortable, and to appease the unaccountable dryness of my throat, I take another long swallow. I daresay my look shows something of the confusion that is closing in about me, for he hastens to continue.

"Having without doubt no other feeling than that of friendliness, and quite, I understand, in the spirit of your own country, you have given Jeanie a very lovely little present. She appreciates and values it highly. Yet—something of course you did not foresee—it carries with it a great deal of embarrassment."

"But—but," I manage, stumblingly, "I do not understand."

"I am sure of that. In short, it has to do with the customs of the country. Here one does not make a gift to another of the opposite sex, unless betrothed, or unless one aspires to betrothe that person."

"Good Lord!" I exclaim. "Was I the cause of her going away—so suddenly?"

"I am afraid so; although innocently. You see, Robert, this is a small, closely knit community—and a bit garrulous too. Without question, your gift is now well known. The people, her neighbors, friends and acquaintances, look upon it in the light of their accepted customs. When presently you go away, and she stays behind, they will not understand; nor will they choose to."

"But, by Jove!" I hear myself saying, with considerable heat, "I will not have her held up in that fashion. She is too fine a girl; she is the finest girl I've ever known—and—and the loveliest too, for that matter."

In my excitement, I have come to my feet. I am grasping something—I believe it must be the glass.

"Furthermore," I rush on, "I'd do anything in the world to save her from it. I've never before given any sort of present to a girl, and I gave her that because I wanted her to have it and because I respect her; and, by Jingo, I'd do it again in a minute—if she'd take it!"

"I am sure," Mrs. McPherson says very gently, and with a long, smiling glance at her husband, "that it will be quite all right."

Her words, and perhaps her tone, quiet me instantly. I regain my seat, and to cover the embar-

[164]

rassment of my outburst, drain the glass which I find
in my hand. Mr. McPherson hastens to refill it, and
his own. He smiles as he raises his glass to mine in
silent toast, and we drink deeply. It seems that the
unwelcome subject is ended, but I cannot dismiss it
altogether.

Although I am sure I am outwardly calm, my
thoughts and my pulses commence racing. I acquire
a strange feeling of belligerence in a worthy cause
against some unknown antagonists. The urge to
strife and rescue, that is the soul of these Scottish
legends, runs hot through my veins. But I set my will
to maintain a proper bearing.

And so considerate and adroit are these good
people, that to relieve my embarrassment, they immediately change the subject of our talk and cleverly
turn the conversation upon myself, and upon their
own situation as well.

It seems that McPherson is out of Oxford, a high
degree man who, as well, sat in his victorious boat
and captained the Rugby varsity. Mrs. McPherson,
I learn, comes from a scholarly Edinburra family.

We are soon again chatting and laughing merrily.
With these confidences, I can hardly refrain from
some of my own, in response to their courteous questioning. I speak, with due modesty I trust, of my
affairs in a business way, and tell of my quarters, my
man and my car. By Jove, I even mention the amount

of my income tax—which conclusively shows the basis of mutual friendliness at which we arrive.

In spite of the momentary *contretemps* of acute embarrassment, it turns out to be altogether a most jolly evening. And that rare Scotch is delicious.

Both courteously see me to the door, and Mr. McPherson even leaves it open for a while, that I may have advantage of the light. When he finally closes it, I have proceeded some distance on the path that curves strangely, and it becomes abruptly very dark. Quite naturally I miss my way a bit, and presently come athwart some rose bushes. But I do not in the least mind the scratches or my rent clothes, for the rare fragrance sets my thoughts peculiarly aglow.

I fight my way steadily onward and after a time encounter the smooth and firm wall of the Inn. With this to guide me in the darkness, I round its four corners and eventually find myself at the porch. It must be later than I had supposed, for there is only one dim light burning above the entrance, and none inside.

Save for my one fall over a chair, which some person has stupidly and thoughtlessly left squarely in the way, I am confident that I gain my room without undue noise. Once there, my eyes light upon the half finished letter to the steamship company.

Instantly I decide that I will have none of it. I

[166]

shall remain and fight it out, although I am a little put to it to understand just what the fight is all about.

At any rate, I seat myself on the bed and proceed to tear the sheet in halves, then into quarters and smaller bits which I toss a few at a time toward the grate. . . .

I expect my day's walk was longer and more fatiguing than I had been aware of; for I allow myself to recline at full length, and I fall asleep.

XV

I AM greatly surprised when I awake after a most refreshing night, to find myself fully dressed. My clothes are in a most deplorable state, with tears and rents in coat and trousers. As I bathe and shave I observe scratches on my hands and some on my cheek.

I am at a loss to understand it. Surely I came directly home from the quiet evening with my friends, and although charging cavalry had a part in my dreams, it isn't conceivable that I could have had such an encounter as would seem to be indicated by the condition of my wardrobe and person.

At breakfast, which I enjoy with a relish I have not known for several days, I chance to overhear Bob Ferguson scolding over a neighbor's cow which he asserts must have wandered into the rose garden during the night. Mildly curious, I strole out to the garden, over my after breakfast pipe, and can quite plainly see the havoc wrought in the meandering path forced by the animal through the bloom laden bushes. . . .

Out of the Rough

In the afternoon, on my way to Sandy's, I take my rent garments to Grannie Robertson who has expressed a desire for light work of that sort. I speak of some slight repairs to be done and do not wait for her to examine them.

Sandy is waiting for me with driver and brassie, and his net of balls at hand. He makes no reference to his absence of two days past, nor of mine yesterday. We go on to the third tee, as before.

He watches me, without comment, as I make several practice swings and drive a couple of balls, which I get off rather creditably. Then he signs to me to rest a bit.

"Ye hae asked me, Robert, how tae keep from daing th' things that are wrang, an' partic'larly tae keep th' body out of th' swing. I hae tauld ye that if ye staund proper, wi' your recht foot weel up tae th' line of your left, if ye hauld your recht elbow tae your side till your han's gang above; then if ye feel your han's start doun first, your body an' recht shouther maun follow an' not get ahead tae spoil your stroke.

"There are ane or twa things mair tae it. Aye, there are a dozen. But th' maist important is, dinna try tae hit too hard till your swing is perfect an' ye nae hae tae think of any pairt of it. Noo ye're maist apt tae forget ane pairt in thinkin' too much of anither.

"Th' second ba' ye just drove, ye tried tae get distance an' forgot your straight left arm on th' backswing. Your baith elbows bent double around your neck; your swing was too short an' nae fu', an' ye tried tae get your han's recht tae th' ba'. Remember this, Robert: Till ye dinna hae tae think of your swing ava, dinna raise your han's higher than your straight left arm will let ye an stop a wee bit at th' top. Try anither th' noo."

I drive several more balls, to better effect.

"Ye're comin,' laddie," Sandy rumbles. "An' mair an' mair ye can think of your timin' an' gettin' th' flick tae your wrists. But dinna press it too fast. Just keep tae that till it's a habit wi' ye an' ye canna dae ane thing different."

Sandy takes the driver from me, and we start toward the fairway.

"Here's ane thing ye can remember, Robert," Sandy says, as we walk slowly along. "If ye're in a match an' mak a bad shot wi' your body in it, th' verra next time dinna raise your left heel from th' grun. Your swing will be shorter, an' ye'll nae get th' distance, but ye'll nae gae sae far wrang an' ye'll come back tae your stroke th' sooner."

In place of going for the balls I have driven, Sandy drops one on the soft, level turf of the fairway and hands me the brassie.

"Th' stroke is like that wi' th' driver," Sandy explains, "an' ye'll nae bother wi' it sae muckle, although it's mair difficult. Your ba' is nae teed up, an' ye maun hit it wi' mair care. For that reason, ye maun gae back verra slow, an' when ye come doun, ye maun feel a' th' way through that your han's are directin' th' club head.

"Anither thing. Dinna hauld in your head that ye maun lift th' ba' from th' grun wi' th' brassie. Th' face of th' club will dae a' that. When ye commence your backswing, Robert, drag your club along th' grass till your han's raise it. Then come up tae th' ba' in th' same way, an' ye'll get it awa. Tak it verra slow th' noo."

I take one or two practice swings, while going over in my mind just what Sandy has told me. When I make the stroke I can truthfully say that for the first time I get off a good brassie shot. In addition to my other faults, the brassie has always been my worst club and in complete discouragement I had come to the point where I rarely used it. Now with my drive fairly well in hand, and closely following Sandy's advice, I do not find any great difficulty.

I make a few more shots, and one is very bad; but that time I am conscious that I hurried the stroke, and furthermore my left arm, on the upswing, was not kept straight. I correct all this on the next try, and Sandy nods his head without comment.

"There's ane thing aboot ye, Robert," Sandy remarks as we strole slowly back toward his cottage, "that's hopefu'. Ye hauld weel in your mind what I hae tauld ye. If ye keep a'ways tae that, stay on your twa feet, nae let your body get in't, I'll mak a gowfer of ye yet. An' ye can dae a' that, Robert," he adds very slowly and deliberately, "if ye nae try tae hit th' ba' too hard."

I think this over for a few paces.

"Sandy," I say, "will you mind telling me again about the timing of the weight shift?"

"Th' proper timing of th' weight shift," Sandy repeats slowly, "is a pairt of th' perfect rhythm of th' stroke. It has a sma' beginning when your han's start doun an' your left heel gaes tae th' grun, but it is maistly done when th' club head hits th' ba' an' your left leg is straight an' firm."

We walk the rest of the way in silence. At his shop door, Sandy turns partly toward me.

"Tomorrer we'll gang tae th' iron; or mair likely tae th' mashie. Guid necht." . . .

I am very restless after dinner. Somehow my room seems too small; the space too confined. I should like to spend the evening conversing with my genial friends of last night; but a call so soon is not to be thought of. Some phases of their talk have been recurring to me, and due to that, no doubt, I am conscious of a feeling of anticipation; but whether it bodes good or evil, it is too vaguely defined for me to surmise. Nevertheless, I am acutely aware of the sensation and it renders me ill at ease.

To distract my thoughts, I take my note book and endeavor to summarize briefly my impressions, up to the moment, of the drive.

I commence with my stance: The left foot almost straight to the ball—at least until I have mastered my balance while making the swing; my right foot well up to the line of my left.

When Sandy made that long drive, I observed that his left foot was pointed well out and that his right was slightly in advance of its line. By the latter I mean a line extended back from the left and paralleling the flight of the ball. This, I understand, is called an open stance, and I have noticed it with other professionals; but they never seem concerned with the matter of balance, which is of most importance to me now.

I must not reach for the ball. Stand as close to it as the club will allow when my hands, dropping naturally, hold the end of the shaft almost against my left leg.

Before starting the stroke, have well in mind that the club head must come down and approach the ball from the inside—that is, from close to the line of my body—go through and beyond it as my right shoulder comes down and allows my right hand and arm to follow after.

Go back on the upswing with timed slowness. Keep the right elbow against my side until my hands at the top of the swing lift it a little higher. On the backswing do not carry my hands around toward my back, but more directly to my side. This, I have thought out, will prevent a twist in my body, which would be bound to give body effort to the stroke when I come down. Make my straight left arm limit the height of my back swing.

Now, as I have timed my upswing, so I will time the downswing. My hands start first, and they start downward and not directly toward the ball. Sandy has told me that the action of the left knee starts simultaneously and the left heel goes to the ground; but I am concentrating on my arms now. The only effort I am to feel is in the back muscles of my left arm, that wrist and thumb, on the shaft, and in the push downward of my right forearm. There must be no sense of other muscular effort.

Timing my downward swing, I increase the speed toward the moment of impact, and toward the bottom of the swing snap my right wrist forward and push my right hand, arm and shoulder down, through and ahead.

While my left arm was straight on the back swing and up to the instant of hitting the ball, it is my right arm now that is straight, and keeps straight

[174]

until the club head goes out and through as far as possible, then whips up overhead.

When I have set down so much, I find that my thoughts tend to wander again and the feeling of vague unrest is returning. I lay my note book aside and presently retire.

XVI

I SURPRISE Bob Ferguson by coming to my
breakfast considerably earlier than my usual
hour. Bob is apparently trying to make amends for
his cool attitude toward me of the past few days; at
least his "guid mornin' " is a bit more cheerful. But
I am deep in my own thoughts, since my early aris-
ing, and do not feel like encouraging conversation.

That sense that I am looking forward to something out of the ordinary has been growing stronger
with me, since my evening with the jovial minister
and his wife, although being of very practical mind,
I am not easily susceptible to outward impressions
and rarely notice what is not fairly obvious. Thus, I
am vaguely aware that I am anticipating, perhaps,
some change in my relations with these good people,
but I do not define what that might be.

I expect it has to do with what Mr. McPherson
explained and my natural feeling of resentment that
unwittingly I have run afoul of these silly conventions, with the risk of being misjudged by all alike.
At least I have begun to suspect that something be-

sides that infernal fog may have influenced the cool
aloofness I have observed in both Bob and Sandy
Macgregor.

On the whole, however, I can scarcely find fault
with Sandy. His instruction of yesterday was as
painstaking as ever; his interest and ambition in my
successful progress as keen. Furthermore, he is con-
tinually giving me tips and suggestions from his long
experience, which are valuable pointers to be treas-
ured and remembered.

I keep always in mind his words, to the effect, that
while he can show me how to play the stroke properly, unless I follow his teaching closely and in no
slightest way depart from it, I can expect no especial
benefit therefrom.

Altogether my purpose here is to learn how to
play the game correctly and make a fairly decent
golfer of myself. From what I have so far accomplished in the eradification of glaring faults in every
part of my swing, I feel confident of success provided I can keep my mind steadily upon it.

Therefore, I do not see why I should concern myself with the idiosyncrasies of a temperamental people or allow the execution of my purpose to be affected in the least.

Yet I do not understand at all my growing rest-
lessness, which this morning amounts to nervous ten-
sion. . . . I expect that I can rid myself of it in my

work of the afternoon. And, by Jove, I almost forgot. He is to show me something of the irons today. Strange, he speaks of an iron and the mashie as if they were not the same. I must remember this.

I am relieved when it is time to set out for my lesson.

As I turn into the little lane and pass Grannie Robertson's, I glance that way and remind myself that on my return I should stop for my suit. It is probably ready for me. . . .

Sandy carries the driver, a mashie and his net of balls as we start for the practice tee. He is taciturn as usual, having nothing to say on our walk across the meadow; but it seems to me, like Bob Ferguson's manner, the look in his keen gray eyes is less forbiddingly dour. In fact, once I thought I saw a gleam of almost amusement as his glance wandered beyond me and back. I wonder why the moods of these two stolid men should be so alike on different days. . . .

Sandy watches me swing, then drive two or three balls, without comment; then takes the driver from me.

"Ye hae seen," he says, "the pairt that th' han's, th' shaft and th' club head play wi' th' woods. Ye understaund recht weel that it is th' head of th' club that sends th' ba' awa. What ye dae in that respect wi' th' wood is anly half what ye maun dae wi' th' iron clubs.

[178]

"Unless it is th' cleek, which ye winna use th' noo, your swing wi' th' irons is shorter, mair compact. Th' shaft is nae sae long, an' ye play th' ba' closer tae ye, wi' mair chance for your recht shouther tae gae doun an' through.

"Wi' a firm grip, your stroke at th' ba' maun be smart an' crisp wi' a sharp follow through. Ye dae it maistly wi' your hands an' wrists, an' th' quicker an' further your recht shouther gaes through after, th' greater will be your distance.

"Dinna mak a swipe at th' ba', Robert. Start your stroke easy an' proper wi' your twa hands comin' doun; then snap your recht wrist an' send your shouther after it. Tak into your mind that, wi' your hands hauldin' an' guidin' it, ye're gaun tae throw your club head at th' ba' an' after it.

"Ane thing mair: The stroke wi' th' iron club is nae heavy or hard. 'Tis a verra easy shot if ye'll let th' club head dae it. Ye maun remember your pivot an' th' easy shiftin' of your weight frae your recht leg tae your left. Ye dinna hae tae squat an' slog at th' ba'. 'Tis a firm, crisp tap wi' th' head of the club gaun recht after it."

Sandy hands me the mashie, while I try assiduously to get clear in my mind all that he has just said. As I understand it I must avoid a swipe, with the hands and wrists stiff with the shaft. I must get a snap into the stroke, which the wrists alone can do,

[179]

and then follow through as fast as I can make my right shoulder come down and go after. I must have the sensation of throwing the club head down and at the ball and following it smartly.

I take my stance to try a swing.

"Where's your ba'?" Sandy asks.

I make a mark in the sand.

" 'Tis nae recht. Ye hae it half way between your twa feet. Ye maun play it aff your left heel."

"Off my left heel?" I repeat, a little bewildered.

"Aye. An' recht in closer tae ye."

I move the club head to the position indicated.

"Your han's are too far back th' noo. Carry them ahead a bit. . . . A wee bit further—just ahead of th' ba'. It'll mak th' stroke easier for ye, an' th' shot straighter. An' it gets your recht shouther doun, where it maun come wi' th' swing."

I make a slow backswing, and Sandy stops me.

"Nae sae far, Robert. A half or three-quarter swing is a' ye'll ever need."

I try another, and when he says nothing, I start my hands down first, then snap my wrists and make my right shoulder go smartly under and through. I repeat this a few times, until I, at least, feel that I have the proper snap and rhythm and follow through. Sandy nods for me to step on the fairway and drops a ball for me to hit.

I take my stance with the ball close and my hands

[180]

in the position he has described. My first attempt is atrocious; for the club head hits the turf inches short of the ball and hardly gets it away at all.

"Nae, nae, Robert. Ye're a' wrang. Ye went at it tae slog it wi' a' your might. 'Tis an easy shot I hae tauld ye; but th' *club head maun dae it*. Anither thing; th' smart follow through wi' th' recht shouther is maist important, but ye were sae anxious tae dae it that ye braced yoursel' backward tae get it in in time. You put yoursel' off balance an' your shouther came doun too soon an' your club hit th' grun. Your shouther maun come doun smart, but it maun come *after* your recht hand in its ain proper time. Then your body will follow ahead wi' it a wee bit an' nae gae back tither way, as ye hae just done it th' noo."

I try a few swings to get the significance of what he has just told me. I find that there is a delicate sequence of timing between the start of the hands, the snap of the wrists and the follow through of the right shoulder, and I see at once that this is their proper order.

Sandy drops another ball, but this time I think only of the correct sequence and not at all of the shot. The result is a distinct surprise to me. I hit the ball crisply and cleanly; the direction is not bad, although not exactly in the line I should like; but with scarcely any sense of effort the distance is greater than I ever expected I could get with a mashie.

Altogether the stroke Sandy has shown me is so totally different from anything I had ever done with that particular club, or with all the iron clubs for that matter, that I give my whole mind to concentrate upon every part of the swing as he has described it. More and more I begin to get the sense of what he means by letting the club head do it, and increasingly I apply this feeling into the effort I give to my hands.

I see clearly that the proper stroke is crisp, hard and firm, with a distinct sense that the club head is going away, after the ball. With each successive shot, my distance increases somewhat. My main difficulty now is that of direction. I seem to hook almost every one. After I hit a dozen balls, Sandy moves to correct this.

"Ye nae hae confidence in your club, Robert." He drops a ball. "Tak your stance."

I move up to it.

"Ye'll see that your club head is closed in. Ye're feart that if ye nae dae that your ba' will gae off tae your recht. Turn it oot till th' face is square at recht angles tae th' direction ye want tae gang, or a wee bit mair. Dinna try tae pull th' ba' in tae your left, but ye maun mak your club gae mair oot an' through th' line of flight. Try it th' noo, Robert, an' dinna gie

[182]

a pull tae your left, but mak th' club gae *a*' th' way *oot*."

I turn the face of my club squarely at right angles, a thing I had never done before, and give all my thought to making the club head go through and out beyond the line of flight. This time the direction is as straight as ever I could wish. I repeat the shot several times with the same satisfactory result and until I feel that I have the sense of this control of direction.

Sandy calls a halt, and we start to gather up the balls.

"Ye maun a'ways hae confidence in your club, Robert," he comments, as we walk along. "When ye hae a bunker ahead an' a wee bit tae your recht, dinna feel that ye maun pull th' ba' awa frae it. Send your club head oot through an' gang after it an' ye'll a'ways hae a straight ba'."

I am too much engrossed in endeavoring to fix steadfastly in my memory all that he has told me today to talk as we cross the meadow to his home. Before he leaves me, however, he turns slowly to face me; and again it seems to me that his ordinarily sober glance holds a strange gleam. But I am too deep in my own cogitation to give it a thought.

"Ye hae done verra weel th' day, Robert, considerin' a'. It is possible that we can gang on tae th' iron—if ye come th' morrow. Guid necht."

[183]

If I come tomorrow! How could I fail to do so! I wonder what he means—unless this is his way of reminding me that I had played truant a few days ago. And of course he wouldn't mention his own absence that had preceded mine.

As I start slowly down the hill I am satisfied that at last I have made really definite progress. Considering that this mashie stroke is entirely new to me, I have made surprisingly few faults, and in fact have adapted myself to the swing quite readily. And it is the correct stroke, the only proper one. I am certain of that; and I am a little elated that I can accomplish it.

I am certain too that I could never have so readjusted myself to this rather definite accomplishment if it were not for my methodical habits of mind. I have perhaps been considered rather slow to think, but that I know is because I have preferred first to analyze the problem before me and to make sure of its import and my own relation with it before acting.

Never have I taken a swift, unpremeditated step. No matter what crisis or exigency has confronted me, I have always paused first to give it due and thorough consideration. The habit is so strong upon me that even now I tell myself that nothing whatsoever will cause me to deviate from it. It has brought me my fair share of success in my business affairs, and now I am convinced that it will prove of equal value

[184]

in becoming a golfer. I am duly thankful that I am that way. . . .

While in the depth of my meditation I have neglected to light my pipe. It also suddenly occurs to me that I have almost passed Grannie Robertson's, with my errand forgotten.

I turn swiftly about—and stop and stare with all my eyes.

Miss Jeanie—Miss Jeanie in all her lovely person is right before me, within arm's length!

XVII

I REACH out and grasp both her hands with my own. I hear my own voice, a little hoarse, scarcely under good control:

"Jean—oh, Jean! Are you back? Jean—I love you! I want to ask you—to marry me!"

She withdraws her hands which I reluctantly yield, steps back a short pace and regards me with her head cocked a little and eyes that are bright and dancing with mischief.

"Fegs!" she says, and laughs, "the man is fair daft wi' his gowf. He comes doun th' hill an' near bumps intae a body an' nae sees them ava; then around he turns an' asks them tae marry wi' him!" She laughs again, wholeheartedly.

"But, Jean—Jean, I was never more serious in my life! I have waited only——"

" 'Haps it may be," she interrupts, in bantering tone, "that master Hale hae taen a fancy tae a bonnie face; for my cousins in Edinburra hae tauld me that I hae grown tae be a recht bonnie lassie."

"Jean, don't torture me! I am serious; I mean it!"

"An' would ye tell me that ye could offer tae marry a wee puir lassie, naithing mair than an innkeeper's daughter?"

"Hang it all, Jean!" I protest, "I don't want to marry Bob Ferguson. It's you, you only I have thought of, and no one else, ever since the first day I came to Elie!"

I advance toward her; she retreats a little hastily, and, fairly convulsed with laughter, holds up a finger and glances askance over her shoulder.

"Losh, master Hale, ye'll hae puir ol' Grannie Robertson arinnin' oot tae see what th' trouble is a' aboot. Let's gang on an' be sensible."

Perforce, I walk on beside her, and at once we reach the turn in the lane and are in the broader road. I glance down and observe that she is wearing the watch on one bare, rounded wrist. I nod toward it.

"Jeanie," I say very soberly, "since I asked you to accept that little gift from me I have learned what it implies in the light of the customs here. I want to tell you that had I known it at the time I still would have asked you to take it."

She is silent for a few paces, and I steal a quick glance at her. I see that her eyes are shining and that she seems with difficulty to control her mirth. It is a bit upsetting.

"An' ye wud hae me believe ye are serious, master

Hale?—— Dinna stop," she adds quickly. "Folk will gawk at us."

"I am utterly serious, Jean," I say quietly. "Will you marry me?"

"Then," she says, with laughter in her voice, "if ye ken sae weel th' customs of th' country, ye should ken that th' man speaks first tae th' lassie's father."

"That," I assure her promptly, "I shall repair immediately."

She laughs outright.

I say no more as we approach the Inn. We come to the point where the two paths separate. Jean starts toward the porch.

I pause. Something beats into my subconscious mind that right here is one of the crises of my life, my whole happiness. Mentally I struggle to bring it into conscious recognition, and a sudden light breaks upon my reasoning.

I realize now, in that instant of reflection, that I have taken for granted Jean and her obvious environment—my first impression was that she was the daughter of the innkeeper, Bob Ferguson—a likable enough but quite ordinary sort of chap. Since that first impression I had thought no more of the matter, although some vague questioning must have assailed my mind at different times. But in all truth, as I have just now told Jean, my entire thought has been for her alone.

[188]

Now, some expression of her face, of her laughing eyes, recalls the many jokes slyly passed at my expense—of course—she could not be of that lowly station——

I turn and take definitely the path leading to the Manse. Jean stops. It seems to me that she looks a little crestfallen; perhaps a bit frightened.

"But where are ye gaun, master Hale?"

"To complete what I have started to do."

"But—I gang here."

"Then I shall see you in a very few moments."

I am around the corner of the Inn, with the Manse before me.

Fortunately my errand consumes but little time, for as I return I meet Jean just emerging to the porch. She has a basket on one arm. Her face is flushed; her eyes do not meet my eager look.

"I canna stop," she says quickly. "I hae a sma' errand tae dae."

"Then I'll go with you." I reach for the basket.

" 'Tis anely for Grannie Robertson. 'Haps ye weel tak it yoursel'. I think your—your clothes are maist ready."

"Then I'll not carry it."

Bob Ferguson appears in the open doorway. He is smiling broadly.

"I'm thinkin'," he calls jovially, "it'll be a recht brecht necht th' necht, Bobbie."

[189]

OUT OF THE ROUGH

Jeanie comes hastily down from the porch, and we walk on together.

I do not speak until we have turned the corner into the little lane. Then I lay a hand on Jeanie's arm and gently stop her when she would continue on.

"Jean," I say, a bit unsteadily, "I have their consent and blessing, and wishes for good luck. Will you make it so? Dear, dear Jean, I love you with all my heart. Will you marry me?"

Her eyes raise slowly to look steadily into mine. They are sober now, and very dark and very deep.

"I know," I tell her quietly, "that I am not all that you deserve. I have not much to offer you except my love and loyalty."

"No," she says slowly, "nothing to offer me, except your clean, wholesome manhood and a heart that is far too big for your own good. . . . Do you really want me, Bobbie?"

Somehow the basket slips to the ground, with a little tinkle of dishes that no one notices. My arms find their way about her slender supple shoulders. Her cool lips are pressed to mine, as fragrant and moist as the rose that fell on my cheek on my first morning's awakening. . . .

We go on to Grannie Robertson's. I wait outside until she rejoins me; then we walk up the little hill, with her arm in mine.

At the top we turn and look over the snug village.
[190]

Out of the Rough

"Jean, Jean," I ask, "why did you ever leave me?"

"I think, Bobbie, we both learned much in my absence." She is silent for a moment, and then says: "Look at that village as it nestles under those great trees; look across the lowlands to the water, and back there to the hills. This is my home. I love every inch of it. I went away, Bobbie, to steel myself still to love it and endure it after you should have gone away."

I go with Jean to the Manse, and after a short while start for the Inn to change, for I am to return for supper.

As I cross the big room toward the stairs, I observe a noisy and very jolly group at the tap. When I enter they are singing the refrain from "The Carles of Dysart," to a great thumping of ale mugs.

> *"Hey, ca' through, ca' through,*
> *For we hae mickle ado . . ."*

There is the big blacksmith, Angus Macbirnie, with whom I have passed a good morning almost every day, Tammie McLean, the sharp-faced postman, Jamie Brown, two others whom I know less well and, of course, Bob Ferguson.

Bob catches sight of me and his voice rolls forth:

"Hey, Bobbie, lad; winna ye join wi' us in th' chorus?"

At that, they all look round, and no doubt due to

the hearty ale of which they are partaking, everyone has a broad smile on his face.

"Thanks," I call back, with a friendly wave of my hand, and without stopping, "I haven't the time now. But make it another round on me."

"Ye're a' recht, mister Hale," roars the mighty voice of the smith. "We're bettin' ye'll tak th' minister ane way or anither." At which there is a general burst of laughter, the sound accompanying me up the stairs. . . .

We are very happy this evening. I have never observed Mr. McPherson in better spirits, while at times his wife is quiet and seems thoughtful. Now that I have the right to look more closely at Jean, I find her even lovelier than ever.

As for myself, I have entered an unsuspected, new world where all is simple and wholesome and good and bright. I can scarcely credit my good fortune.

We have serious matters as well to discuss. It seems that Jean has been offered a position on the University faculty, at Edinburra—for the life of me, I cannot now call it anything else. It is in the department of foreign languages, her father explains, and her new duties are supposed to begin in the Fall.

Of course it is out of the question. I couldn't think of returning to America alone, and I can hardly give myself more than the month and a half yet remaining to me.

With that matter settled in happy agreement—the import of which sends a flush to Jeanie's cheeks, puts me into a state of mild trepidation and leaves us all momentarily quiet—Mr. McPherson must have his little joke.

"Oh, Jean," he says across to her, "I expect you will be greatly disturbed over the serious damage that has been done to your roses. Ferguson is under the impression that one of the neighbor's cows wandered into the garden during the night. Upon my word, she made a path, if not exactly straight, at least right through it."

Jean, laughing a little in spite of herself, shakes a finger at him.

"From now on," she says, "please remember, Bobbie is under my care. He was too polite to refuse what you no doubt pressed upon him, and how could he know that one shouldn't mix Scotch with a half dozen mugs of ale?"

Mrs. McPherson also comes to my rescue with the assertion of her belief that it was really a cow, for "certainly nothing else could possibly have done it." At this, the minister laughs uproariously again and again.

When his wife and daughter finally quiet him, he turns to a new tack.

"It is the very first time in all my experience," he says in sober voice, "that I ever have heard of a young man wanting to marry a girl for the sake of the grand old game of golf."

"Now just for that," Jean answers him spiritedly, "I will help Bobbie every single day, and when you play that match you will be the one down."

"Hum," says the minister, with twinkling eyes, "now that is a real handicap. What odds are you giving me, Bobbie? Say, about three bisques?"

"No," I say, with all the confidence in the world. "We're playing even; but I'll stake a dinner for four on it."

"Done!" says the minister heartily. Then adds: "I must see if Ferguson can possibly get you in some pheasant from the uplands. I am especially fond of them."

"Bobbie," says Jean, and extends her hand. "Let's beat him!"

"If it is in me, we'll do it," I assure her, thrilling to her strong grip. "Do you mean it? Will you really help?"

"Oh, ho!" says the minister. "Little did I imagine I was furthering a conspiracy against me when I telephoned word of your urgent need."

And now it is Jeanie's turn really to blush.

"Of course I will help you," she says, a little hastily. "Shall we begin tomorrow?"

"Let's say day after tomorrow," I suggest, with an idea in mind that happily had occurred to me

[194]

while dressing. "I can arrange for a car. I was hoping that the four of us might motor up to Edinburra tomorrow."

The minister and his wife agree that it can be done, while Jean glances at me with quick suspicion. Then Mr. McPherson commences to chuckle.

"I see very well," he says, with an attempt to appear serious, "that I shall have to polish up my game; for Bobbie here hasn't forgotten even his very first lesson."

XVIII

NOW how could that canny old Scot, Sandy Macgregor, possibly suspect that I might not appear for my customary lesson on the following day? When I left him, greatly encouraged over my initial attempts with the mashie, I had every intention of doing so, but it is two days later when Jean and I walk up the hill to his modest cottage.

There are many things I want to ask Jean, although for the past day we have been busy on affairs not strictly related to golf. I have, however, as well as possible made mental note of them intending to bring them up at the proper time.

Sandy meets us with a broad smile for my companion and a long, rather searching look at me, in which, save for the twinkle in his keen eyes, I can find little expression. He makes no reference whatever to the matter of such great importance to us, although I daresay by this time he knows all about it.

Jean stands a little in the background as I take a few practice swings and get off several drives from the tee. Sensible of the impulse of her presence to get distance, nevertheless I resist it, and the result is as creditable as I dare hope.

We step to the fairway and I repeat the performance with the brassie. My first stroke is very bad. I drive the ball into the turf and it goes only a few yards. Sandy explains the trouble.

"Ye hae come recht doun on th' ba', Bobbie, instead of comin' up tae it along th' grun. Ye tried tae mak your hands gae straight for't. Ye maun let your full dounswing tak care of that."

I try again, and this time concentrate on the first downward movement of my hands at the full extension of my straight left arm. I get a clean hit with both good distance and direction. It seems to me that on my first attempt, my left elbow unconsciously bent at the top of my back swing, causing my hands to cut across the arc of the full downswing, with the effect that Sandy made clear.

"Wi' th' brassie," Sandy comments, "ye maun a'ways hae in your mind that th' han's are guidin' th' club head up tae th' ba'. It's a mair carefu' shot than th' driver, as I hae tauld ye. Anither thing. Hae ye ever seen a bull charge, Bobbie?"

"A bull charge?" I repeat, puzzled as to what that might have to do with golf. "Once, but I do not understand. . . ."

"Na?" he asks dryly. "Ne'erth'less, there's a point in't for ye. When a bull hooks, he closes his een. Lots of folk dae th' same thing, when they hit something hard, or pull a trigger, or drive a gowf ba'. Keep your een open, an' recht on th' ba'. After she's weel awa ye can leuk up an' watch her drop; but ye canna shut your een wi' th' brassie wi' guid success."

"But, Sandy, do you mean to say that I closed my eyes on the shot?"

I hear Jean chuckling behind me.

"I am tellin' ye nae tae dae it," is the most direct answer Sandy will give me. "Ane time I hae seen a man drive a long ba' blindfold, but ye canna learn th' game that way, Bobbie."

Now here is something I should never have suspected; and I'm not certain whether Sandy is joking, or taking this way of warning me against the danger. It seems impossible that I could have closed my eyes on the shot; yet, as I recall the exact moment of impact, when I put every effort into the stroke—— I wonder?

"If ye pull your een awa frae th' ba' too soon," he says, dryly, "it's as muckle bad as if ye shut your een. Keep your een recht there an' watch th' club head hit th' ba'. It's a guid rule for everra shot, Bobbie, an' it's maist important wi' th' brassie and wi' th' iron."

Sandy allows me only three balls with the brassie; then gives me the mashie.

I pause and idle with the club while I run over in
[198]

my mind all that Sandy has shown me of the stroke that is so new to me.

I remember that above all I am to have the sense that the club head is doing the work, as Sandy expresses it, and the feeling that, with a firm grip on the shaft, I am throwing it down and after the ball. And perhaps of equal importance is to send the head through and beyond the line of flight, which can only be accomplished by making my hands go out as far as possible and my right shoulder to go under and through quickly enough so that it will not retard my hands and pull them in too soon.

I recall the position of the ball, fairly close in and off my left foot, and my stance with my hands up to or a little in advance of it, which brings my right shoulder down in position. I have observed also that in this position, my wrists are already cocked for the snap which I must give to them as the ball is hit, imparting a crispness to the shot.

Apparently I take considerable time in my mental résumé, for Sandy remarks to Jean:

"He is a carefu' laddie, is Bobbie, an' that's a guid sign."

When I come to hit the several balls Sandy drops for me, in my anxiety to get a proper follow through at first I have a little difficulty with my right shoulder getting into the stroke too soon. After a bit, however, I acquire a better sense of the timing of

[199]

hands, arms and shoulder, with more satisfactory result.

"Th' mashie is a verra usefu' club," Sandy comments, as he takes it from me. "The stroke wi' it is easy an' compact, an' th' balance is firm. When ye come tae learn your ain distance wi' it, Bobbie, ye can control your shot an' play for th' pin everra time. Soon nae doot ye'll be takin' a little turf wi' your mashie, but ye maun everra time play your stroke through.

"An' remember this: it's nae guid tae try tae overplay any club beyond its ain proper distance. If it's a longer shot than ye can get wi' th' mashie wi'out pressin', tak anither club that has nae sae muckle loft. If it's a half mashie, use your mashie niblick, an' if ye're recht close tae th' green, wi' a trap tae get ower, tak your niblick."

"But I thought that the niblick is only for getting out of sand traps, deep bunkers or heavy grass, Sandy."

"Th' niblick," says Sandy, "is a recht guid club for a short pitch tae a fast green, but ye maun first learn its distance on a fu' swing an' a half swing, an' ye maun hit th' ba' recht, wi' your stroke gaun a' th' way through.

"There's ane thing I want tae tell ye, Bobbie, that ye dinna dae wrang th' noo, but ye might if ye're nae carefu'. It's important in a' strokes but it's maist

[200]

important wi' th' shots ye play clean off th' grun an'
nae teed up. Ye maun never scootch doun tae your
shots. Sae lang as ye shift frae your straight recht
leg tae your straight left leg, ye'll never dae it. If ye
bend your knees taegither an' come doun on your
legs when ye hit at th' ba', ye'll spoil your shot an'
ye'll foozle a mashie awfu'."

Sandy hands me an iron which I observe is a number two.

"Yon's a difficult club, Bobbie," he remarks, "an'
th' number one is mair sae. Ye canna play it just like
th' mashie. Ye canna gie it a' th' wrist ye gie tae
that, but ye maun gie it some, an' ye maun get your
shouther in after it an' send th' club head oot. It's
mair like th' stroke wi' th' brassie, which ye play wi'
a slower upswing an' a mair carefu' dounswing than
ye dae wi' th' driver. Ye maun hit th' ba' sharp an'
crisp, and it's th' han's an' wrists an' arms an' th'
club head that dae it a'."

I know, of course, that the shaft of the iron is
slightly longer than that of the mashie and I make
allowance for it as I take my stance; too much so,
apparently, for Sandy tells me to play it closer. I
take the same position as for the mashie, with the
ball opposite my left heel and my hands well ahead.
Then I try several practice swings to get the feel of
the club.

I hit the first ball fairly clean, for I keep in mind

what Sandy said about shifting from one straight leg to the other, which I understand, of course, preserves the proper distance from my shoulders down my straight arms and the shaft to the ball when it is hit. I also remember to watch, with wide open eyes, the club head hit the ball. The distance, however, is not good and the ball goes off to the right.

"Ye nae let th' club head dae a' its work," Sandy comments, "for ye swiped at it wi' your wrists maistly stiff. An' anither thing, Bobbie. When ye face your club square, or a little mair oot, an' hae your hands ahead, ye maun drive th' head *oot* across th' line. Mak your hands gang *oot*, laddie, an' your recht shouther gang after an' a' th' way through. Ye hae pulled it in too soon th' noo."

The next time, I think not of distance at all but concentrate on getting a clean, crisp hit, with the club head going right out beyond the line of flight and all the way through, as Sandy has admonished me. When I finish, I note to my keen satisfaction that, while my feet, slightly turned, are still firm, my right shoulder is straight ahead. And again I prove that curious axiom: "The easier you hit it, the farther it goes."

It is a difficult club, this number two, as Sandy has well advised; and all my shots are not as good as I should like them to be. But when I finally get a low, clean, hard shot, with plenty of carry and run and in excellent direction, Sandy calls it enough for the day, and we start to gather up the balls.

"You have a very good swing, Bob," Jean comments, as we cross the little meadow.

"Do you really think so?" I exclaim, delighted beyond measure. "But you must have noticed some faults, haven't you?"

Jean quickly presses my arm, and I understand instantly that she prefers not to discuss the matter before Sandy. In fact, she turns toward him with a question.

"Frankly, Sandy, do you think Bobbie has a chance against my father?"

Sandy shakes his head; but there's a twinkle in his shrewd gray eyes.

"I'll nae say he has nae a guid chance; but th' minister is ane stubborn fechter—nane better. If he had minded as weel as ye hae, Jeanie, there's few could worst him hereaboot. But he would gang off on his ain, an' verra frequent he has trouble in keepin' on th' course."

"But we must beat him, Sandy!"

"Weel—we'll dae a' mortal can dae wi' Bobbie, an' leave it tae Providence an' Tammie. Half a match is a matter o' temperrament; an' when it comes tae soothin' a gowfer, Tammie is verra guid. There's ane thing ye can hauld in mind, Bobbie. When ye hae a match agee a guid man, dinna think of ane thing else than just th' shot ye're makin'."

Jean gives me a quick look and a smile, and I know what value she places on this sage advice.

Sandy stops before his door.

"Ye can bring your ain clubs th' morrow, Bobbie. I'll hae a leuk at them."

He regards us both and seems in no hurry to leave, so we wait.

"Bobbie," he says finally, turning more directly to me, "when ye caught that grand fesh th' first day oot, I said ye're lucky, but I dinna ken ava how awfu' lucky ye are. Laddie, put this in your pow. Nae man is guid enough for Jeanie th' warl ower, but if I dinna think ye're as guid as maist, I'd hae a word tae say aboot it."

He is very serious in saying this; then he beams upon us with a warmth of which I did not suspect him capable.

"Guid necht tae ye baith!"

He waves a hand, and the little doorway swallows his huge shoulders.

XIX

J EANIE says that it is perfectly shameful to expect a girl to get ready for her wedding in a
little over a month's time, and in addition prepare
everything for a voyage across the sea and a new
home on the other side. Still she sets about it all as
if it were not altogether an unhappy task, and in
spite of her preoccupation shares most of the days
with me.

Moreover, she is on the links with me on every
possible occasion, although she promises that after
"the match" is over, I may expect nothing further of
the sort.

Therefore, on my first practice day with her alone,
I decide to glean from her a fuller explanation of
some points at which Sandy has hinted and of those
which I am not certain that I thoroughly understand.

From the very first I have recognized that Sandy
is sparing of words and does not relish repeating an
explanation. I am quite sure that such progress as
I have made under his tuition is due to two facts:

First, to the best of my ability I have adhered strictly to every bit of instruction he has given me. Second, practically every evening, up to the time of that blessed fog, I have spent in writing down or pondering all that he has told me on the particular day, transferring it, as far as possible, into language of my better understanding, and then putting the result into actual practice.

Still there are several matters left unsettled. Furthermore I am curious to learn in just what manner Jean acquired her marvellously effective form. I want to comprehend how she, a slender girl, although lithe and strong, can so often outdrive her stalwart father and invariably improve on his direction.

Sandy is allowing me to use some of my own clubs. He has changed the weight of my brassie to match the driver of his that I have been using, and is holding out my own driver. I have also in my bag this morning my own numbers two and three, his mashie and mashie niblick and my niblick and putter.

He seems a little grateful that he can turn me over to Jean; he says that he has some work of his own on which he wants to get busy. We do not bother even to take a caddie, but go to the links alone.

In place of stepping directly to the tee, I lead Jean aside to a little bank where a maple casts a bit of shade. She seats herself on the grass and after filling my pipe I drop down beside her. I expect she is conscious of the admiration in my eyes—for in all truth I have never seen anyone so beautiful—for her own eyes are downcast and she pretends to study the ring, on one slender finger, which we found in Edinburra.

Finally, she looks up quickly, with her bright smile, and shakes a finger at me.

"You know, Bobbie, you want to talk about golf."

I relight my pipe, which has gone out. Then I tell her of all the faults in the game which I had brought with me.

"Tell me, Jean," I ask, "how did you first get the sense of having all power in the stroke given by your hands and arms alone? You give not the slightest indication of body effort."

She laughs a little.

"I imagine, Bobbie, that all your troubles started when you tried to play the game before you really knew what it was all about. Probably you tried to get long drives and make a low score when you had little if any idea in what manner the stroke should be made."

"That is absolutely true," I agree. "Furthermore, like almost every boy in America, I was in other sports, particularly baseball, and went at golf in the same way."

"Fortunately for me," she says, "when I was a wee bit of a girl, father turned me over to Sandy. And the first thing he did was to make me half-sit on a tee box and swing a club with my arms, where I couldn't move my body at all.

"He didn't take me fishing, or have me thresh wheat, but he explained very carefully just how the club head must snap into the ball and stay behind it until it has flown away.

"When he was satisfied that I could control my muscles so that my arms and wrists made the whole effort, he let me stand away from the tee box. Then he took my club head and moved it slowly in the only path it can go in order to hit the ball properly and stay squarely behind it for the vital instant of time. That is the all important point.

"He explained the shifting of weight, from the right leg to the left; he showed me just how my body should pivot, my right shoulder go up and come down and under to follow the hands through and out. He repeated this over and over until my muscles responded to make the club travel in its only one proper path and I knew no other habit.

"It seems to me now that he spent months at this. I am sure that I didn't try to play a full hole for a long while. Then I was away at school, but every Summer I took it up again. When I grew old enough, I commenced to think it out for myself.

"I remember that I used to consider the arc of my swing as a plane, like the flat surface of a round table. To get the upright swing, which he wanted me to adopt, I had only to tip my table 'way, 'way over until it was at an angle of about thirty degrees from the vertical."

I ponder this until I get the sense of what she means. I think it will help to keep the club head from dropping down at the top of the backswing and to finish out and high.

"You have a good swing now, Bobbie," she breaks into my thoughts, "and very few if any of the faults you have described. Your swing is not yet free; you give the impression of holding in a little and taking care, and that is just what you should do until the right habit is thoroughly established.

"A little later, as it was with me, you will get a better sense of the timing which gives a crispness to the shot and distance; but that is the final touch and you should work toward it slowly, as you are now doing."

"Tell me, Jean," I ask, after a moment of silence, "do you know what Sandy means by his reference to his own idea of the stroke?"

"I think I do," she answers slowly. "For one thing, Sandy is an ardent fisherman; that is, a fly caster. I believe he has the same sense with his club that he has with the rod. He can bring it down solely with his arms, then at just the right moment, flick it through with his wrist. That means all the difference

[209]

between a stiff-armed swipe and a snappy hit. Of course the pivot of his body, the following through with his shoulder is automatic. For another thing ____"

"Let me see if I have guessed that," I interrupt, suddenly recalling my thought on the morning when I smashed the rose bowl and Bob Ferguson interrupted me. "I think it has to do with the question of which arm has the greater control."

Jean nods her lovely head, in alert interest.

"I believe," I say slowly, "that his theory is that outside the effort given by the heel of the right hand as the downswing starts, the left arm is in control up almost to the instant when the ball is hit, when the right hand takes control to guide the club, to snap the head into the ball and to push the club head through and away out. The right can carry it out only when the right shoulder does not lag but comes right through after it."

Jean claps her hands delightedly.

"Bobbie, you are a marvel! I don't know how you ever thought it out, but I believe that is exactly what Sandy thinks. However, it takes such a delicate balance of mind, or rather, such a perfect coördination of mind and muscle that I expect few people would want to bother about it. Now, sir; are you going to practice? And one thing—remember; don't let father cause you to overswing. He puts such mighty effort

[210]

into his drive, that it will be a real temptation. Promise?"

"I promise."

The promise is properly sealed, and we start on what is to me a most satisfactory hour of practice. . . .

When we pick up the last ball, Jean pauses.

"You know, Bob," she says, musingly, "when my timing is right, my shots going well and I am getting distance, I have a certain sense or feeling of the stroke I want to tell you about.

"I imagine my body working on an axis, that is the vertical center of my weight and muscular power, like a straight steel rod. All parts of my body have different work to perform on this axis: First one then the other leg is straight or bent; my hips turn in a horizontal plane; my shoulders rotate, or pivot, at a somewhat acute angle; my arms swing back and up, and down and up; my head alone remains in the same relative position with the ball.

"As I say, when my stroke is right, all these parts doing their several duties properly and in right time, I have the sense that this central axis pushes forward with the impetus given to the hit and helps to carry it on.

"It is a strange and fantastic idea, I know, and a dangerous one to play with at times, for if I confuse parts of my body, such as the shoulders, with what I call the axis, I am apt to get my body ahead of the stroke. It is only when everything is going perfectly that I can use this idea to advantage, and then I have gotten my longest distances.

"You can think about it, Bob, for I know you like to ponder over your golf; but don't try to put it into application just yet. . . . Come on; we must hurry home."

Another day, when Jean avows that the seamstress will not excuse her, Sandy takes two putters and a pocket full of balls, and we go to the nearest green.

"Th' matter of puttin', Bobbie," he says, "is a verra simple ane, but I dinna doot there are mair styles o' puttin' than gowf players, for maist puir gowfers change their style everra time they miss th' hole.

"There are twa things aboot 't: the matter of sightin' an' th' matter of hittin'. Everra man must judge for himsel' how he can staund th' steadiest— for ye maunna move your body when ye putt—an' how he can sight th' best; but if ye hae your ba' behind ye, that is near your recht foot, ye canna weel judge where th' hole is.

"Your ba' will gang where ye hit it; I'm speakin' th' noo of a level green. If ye hae your line frae ba' tae hole recht, if ye hauld th' face of your club square at recht angles tae that line, an' then swing your putter back, intae th' ba' an' ahead wi't recht

[212]

along that line, th' ba' maun gang tae th' hole, barrin' a trick o' th' green.

"Th' maist important thing then is tae mak your club travel back an' forrard along that straight line. If ye swing your body wi' th' stroke, ye'll pull th' putter around. If your wrists dinna work taegither, that is, bendin' in th' same direction, ye'll dae it too.

"Here, Bobbie, open your twa hands an' place your palms taegither. Bend your wrists th' noo. Ye see—they're working taegither like twa hinges ane atop anither. An' that is a' recht. Tak your club th' noo an' hauld it wi' your wrists opposite ane anither like that."

Sandy extends the shaft of the putter and I grasp it, with care that my wrists are in the same relative position as when my palms were together.

"Waggle it."

I do, and observe that my wrists bend in exactly the same direction, and not one away from the other.

"That is guid," Sandy comments, "an' th' way it should be. Hae ye any fav'rite stance for your puttin', Bobbie, whaur ye can secht th' best?"

"None particular. I wish you would give me one."

"I can gie ye ane, an' ye can try it an' see how ye mak oot. Th' first thing is th' steady balance, frae whaur ye can best see th' line. Put your heels taegither, wi' your left foot pointin' straight tae th' hole. Bend baith knees a little. Rest your recht elbow

[213]

on your hip. See th' noo if ye can swing your putter
back an' forrard, wi' your wrists anely, in th' ane
straight line."

I try it and Sandy seems satisfied.

He drops a ball at my feet and steps away from
me a distance of about ten feet.

"Face me, Bobbie," he says, "an' send your ba'
here."

He holds his putter between his feet. I change my
position toward him, with my left foot pointing to
the shaft of his club. Careful that my blade is at
right angles to the line, I tap the ball to him. He
sends it back, in such a way I have to change position
and take my stance anew. We repeat this performance a half dozen times until I have a better sense
of the easy, yet controlled stroke he has shown me.

"Nae, Bobbie," he says at last, "dinna tap th' ba'
an' stop your club. Let th' club travel along wi' th'
ba' a wee distance."

This brings better results, and he takes me up
within three feet of the hole. Each time he places a
ball so that I have to change my position. When I
drop three in succession, he moves me back to six
feet; then ten, fifteen, and for one putt twenty, before he pauses.

"Ye'll hae tae work oot your ain judgment of distance tae your stroke, Bobbie, but there are twa
things I can tell ye. First, mak everra putt carefu'.

Try everra time tae drop it in th' hole. Ye maun never tak a hurried, careless putt, or ye'll lose your sense o' touch.

"Aboot direction. When ye are close, whaur ye can see baith your ba' an' th' hole taegither, ye know th' exact line. When ye are awa whaur ye can see anely ane at a time, square your club head first, then leuk at th' hole an' draw your een slow straight back tae your ba'. That gies ye your line an' ye maun remember it, as if it were drawn recht on th' grun.

"When ye hae th' line, leuk again at th' hole, an' when ye leuk back tae your ba', hauld in your mind just where th' hole lies an' putt for 't.

"When ye hae a slopin' green or a rollin' ane, ye maun mak allowance for 't, which anely practice will gie ye. But ye can hauld in mind that a slow ba' will roll off on a slopin' green muckle mair than a fast ane; that is, when th' ba' is near th' hole an' gaun slow, it will roll off mair than when ye hae started it."

Sandy pockets the balls, stands erect and sweeps the links with his keen eyes.

"We hae anely a few days th' noo tae th' match, Bobbie. Ye maun practice your puttin' everra chance ye get. Ye hae a guid touch on' th' greens, laddie, an' I'm nae worrit aboot 't, but ye maun tak your time on everra putt an' mak everra putt count. An' remember, it's muckle better tae be a wee bit ower than awa short." [215]

XX

JEAN and I spend the morning on the links where I take several shots with the number two iron, then practice approaches to a green, first with the mashie, then with the mashie niblick.

"I have found it a very helpful rule," she says, after watching me for a while in silence, "to start my backswing, particularly with all iron clubs, very slowly. Even though for the past two years or so I have felt rather certain of my stroke and the result to follow, I have kept to this rule, and having established the habit, it kills any tendency ever to hurry my shot."

I have observed that Jeanie always corrects me in this indirect fashion. Sometimes I wish she would come right out and say: "Bob, you put a little body into it that time," or "you didn't finish your swing; you stopped it too soon," or "you didn't carry your club through and out far enough and your shoulder was slow in coming after it."

But, no, bless her heart, she corrects my fault as if she herself had made it. In a way it is flattering, for it seems to say that in her eyes I can do no wrong, and certainly it is the least disconcerting method of

[216]

setting one right that I have ever experienced. My immediately following shot is always better, and I rarely forget the point she thus emphasizes.

I make several clean hits with the mashie, but my placing is poor. Either the direction is off, or my distance is too little or too great.

"There is a strange thing about a shot, Bob," she says, when I pause, "which is more or less psychological. After I learned just how the stroke is made—say with the mashie which you are using—and could make it, I discovered two very important things. The first is what I spoke of—not hurrying. The second is this: Before making the stroke, I fixed very carefully in my mind both the direction and the distance, right to the pin. I could still look at my ball and feel exactly where the pin was and the spot where I should land to run up to it. I knew too, beforehand, just what effort the particular shot required. Then—I made the stroke with all the confidence in the world that it would be right. I firmly believe that confidence does everything for one."

Jean laughs—a low, musical sound that always thrills and delights me.

"You may not believe it, Bob, but when I first went into matches and was not at all sure of myself, I would worry and fret that an important shot might go wrong. And it invariably did."

Right then and there I put this idea to the test,

[217]

summoning whatever faith in myself I can muster, and I cannot say that it is altogether real and convincing. Nevertheless, the result gives me greater confidence in my next effort, and after a very few shots I have something I had never even dreamed of possessing—a feeling, a confidence that I can place the ball approximately where I want it to go.

It may seem a small thing; but to me it is the greatest single stride I have yet made. I have a sense of mastery that is incomparable.

I am fairly bubbling with enthusiasm and gratefulness to my dear Scottish lassie, as we jokingly make our way back to luncheon. . . . I seem to be expected each day at the Manse for luncheon, and again in the evenings.

The thought that very shortly now we shall not have to separate at all fills me with a strange happiness. I do not seem in the least acquainted with my former, isolated self. And further, I am aware of an impression that all things here have given me something in addition even to my unsuspected happiness and beyond my newly acquired knowledge of this sterling game.

In the afternoon, dear Jean is again busy.

Sandy takes me into what appears to me a quite formidable sand trap, although its banks are neither very abrupt nor especially high. We have our niblicks.

[218]

OUT OF THE ROUGH

"Dinna be feart, laddie," he tells me, "of your traps or your bunkers. Ance ye are in them, there's ane thing tae dae—get oot. An' ye can dae it everra time—if ye think anely of that ane thing.

"There are twa ways tae dae it, dependin' if ye are a guid gowfer an' verra sure of yoursel'. Ane way is tae tak an easy stroke and hit th' ba' fairly clean, maistly like a chip shot. I dinna recommend it tae ye th' noo. Tither way, an' th' sure way, is tae tak a strong shot an' tak a niblick fu' of sand an' th' ba' taegither. An' wi' baith, ye maun swing your club a' th' way through."

He drops a ball on the level surface at the bottom of the trap.

"Try it th' noo, Bobbie; an' remember it's your regular niblick stroke played slow an' a' th' way through."

I step up to the ball, and glance once at the top of the bank.

"Na, na, laddie. Back a wee bit. Frae th' level or on an up slope, play it off your left foot. Hit th' sand just behind your ba' an' mak your club gang through."

I make the stroke, and put the strength of my hands and arms into it, for I am determined to dig out some sand, exactly as Sandy has told me. There is a great cloud of dust and flying sand. I keep my

[219]

head resolutely down; but the ball has disappeared. I glance up where the cloud is settling.

" 'Tis on th' green, laddie," Sandy rumbles. "Try anither."

With that marvelous sense of confidence, which Jean has this morning given me, I loft several out of the pit without a single mishap. Then Sandy tries me on one or two on the rising bank nearest the green, and finally takes me to the opposite bank where the slope is downward. Under Sandy's direction, I play the ball farther back toward my right foot. It is very difficult at first, but soon I observe that the one and only thing is to make the hit correctly and go all the way through with the swing.

"When ye come tae play th' minister," Sandy tells me, as we clamber to the green for some putting, "ye'll tak just this shot, wi' th' sand, an' nane ither. If ye hae a high steep bank afore ye, Bobbie, ye can lay your club back a wee bit—bein' carefu' that ye nae slice under th' ba' an' nae tak it ava—an' instead of carryin' your han's awa oot, stop them at your shouther an' mak your club head come up sharp. That'll raise yer ba' straighter. Can ye remember it, laddie?"

"Sandy," I tell him very seriously, "I have not forgotten one little point you have told me since we first started together, and I shall not forget this."

The next day Sandy lets me play several full holes,

interspersed with practice shots with brassie, mashie niblick or whatever club I may not have played to his satisfaction.

I observe that Sandy walks very briskly to the ball, but when up to it makes sure that I take plenty of care in the preparation of the shot. I do not mean that he wants me to hang over the ball. Quite on the contrary; when I have determined distance and direction, judged the stroke to be made and taken my proper stance, then, without undue delay, my deliberate backswing commences. I watch him very closely and adopt this method as a habit to be fixed and retained.

"Sandy," I remark, as we leave the third tee, "if I had avoided that trap on the first, I might easily have saved two strokes on the hole."

"Ye canna gang back an' play your approach ower again, laddie. What's behind ye, guid or bad, leave behind ye. Your anely worry th' noo is th' shot comin' up."

* * *

The following day Jeanie comes with me, for the short hour or so she can spare. Tammie, the sharp-faced, old caddie is waiting with my bag; and Sandy tells me that I am to play nine holes, without any practice between. As we start off, I notice that he carries a driver and two other clubs.

I admit that I am a little nervous on the first

drive, but on the whole I play the first two holes fairly creditably. I feel that I owe it to Jeanie to play my strokes with all the confidence in the world. At the same time I am careful not to hit too hard.

Going up to the third, Sandy precedes me and sends away a tremendous ball. I can almost feel the power he puts into it; and it is done with such consummate ease and sense of control that I am conscious of an irresistible urge to match it.

In stepping to my ball, however, I chance to glance at Jean and observe that she is frowning slightly. Instantly comprehension comes to me. Deliberately, I take a very moderate swing, and as the ball gets away straight, I hear Sandy grunt, involuntarily, with what I assume is satisfaction.

As we leave the fourth green, I count up my strokes and to my surprise find that I am only one over fives. It occurs to me that if I can keep up the same pace, I shall do the nine in excellent figures. Walking on to the tee, I look over the fairway before me to the far green and estimate the strokes that I should take to get home. Then I step up to address the ball.

"Bobbie," Sandy calls to me quietly, "what club hae ye in your han's?"

I look down in surprise, then glance at his gray eyes that are regarding me so shrewdly.

"Why—the driver, of course."

OUT OF THE ROUGH

"Then 'tis th' driver ye're playin' th' noo; nae th'
iron, nae th' mashie niblick, nae th' putter. They'll
come in a' guid time; but keep your mind anely on
th' ane club ye hauld in your hands, whatever it is,
an' play th' stroke wi't."

Tomorrow is the big match. As usual I come over
to the Manse right after dinner. Mr. McPherson is
in fine fettle. Several times he asks me, very seriously,
if I have ordered the pheasant and if I feel quite certain Bob will have them in time. He promises that he
will come to the Inn to supervise their roasting, as
he is very particular that they should be done just
right.

He assures me, also, that every man, woman and
child able to walk in The Elie will be on hand. Then
he sighs and expresses his deep concern over so many
of the poor people who cannot afford to lose even
a farthing; although for the life of him he cannot
understand how any bets could be made, to say nothing of the whole town gambling, for, he adds: "It
takes two sides to make a bet."

I am really looking forward with tremendous interest, and some perturbation, to the morning, and
there are many things I should like to discuss with
him. But this evening Jean seems filled with curiosity
over our home across the seas and simply will not
speak of anything else.

When I leave, she accompanies me to the door.

With the memory of her dear arms around me and the swift touch of her warm lips on mine, I find, on my return to my solitary room, that I am quite unable, as I intended, to review carefully every single stroke in the whole bag of clubs.

XXI

I CANNOT avoid the thought that if anyone were so bold as to plan the town bank robbery, the best way to gain freedom from interference would be to set up a golf match.

As Jeanie, Mr. McPherson, Sandy, our two caddies and myself walk toward the first tee, I am quite ready to believe that the whole town is on the links awaiting us. Perhaps I exaggerate; but I have always been sensitive to crowds if I were apt to attract attention. I am not particularly subject to self conscious embarrassment; still I keenly dislike making a show of myself, and since awakening this morning, notwithstanding my valiant effort to rout it, a suspicion has been lurking in the back of my mind that I might do that very thing.

Everyone in the party, with the possible exception of myself, seems in genuinely good spirits. I attempt a jollity equal to that of the rest, but I must admit, as we draw near that crowd, my laugh sounds a bit hollow in my own ears.

Jeanie, bless her heart, senses my tendency toward nervousness, for, as we walk alone for a moment, she tells me that the match is nothing; I am merely out to practice my strokes. The fact that the number of strokes I practice are to be matched against those of her father is a matter of indifference, at least so far as she is concerned, for she knows how well I can play.

That helps, and I feel a return of the confidence that seemed on the point of deserting me entirely. Then when Mr. McPherson and I are fairly on the tee, he insists on shaking hands, to the noisy amusement of the onlookers, and gives me a great clap on the shoulder.

Many voices call a greeting to the popular clergyman, who is laughing heartily. As the shouts cease, one pipes out:

"Ye maun tak it serious, minister; our siller is on ye!"

To which the great voice of the blacksmith, Macbirnie, roars:

"Na a' of us, Jamie. Ma wad's on master Hale! He's ane aboon afore they start!"

At this, the genial clergyman waves an arm and laughs until he has to wipe his eyes.

We each insist the other take the honor. Finally we toss a coin, and it falls to my call. Only then, Tammie approaches me with my bag. He is slow in drawing out the driver.

"Be cauld, master Hale," he whispers. "Tak this

Be cauld, master Hale.

first ane as easy as ye ken how. Dinna try fer any distance ava."

I give all my will power to follow this sage advice and overcome an impulse, which I daresay is due to nervousness, to hit with all my might. Really, my drive is quite respectable even for distance and is squarely in the fairway.

Mr. McPherson follows me with a tremendous swipe, sending the ball fifty yards beyond mine, although hooked to the left on to the edge of the parallel fairway.

"We're off, laddie," he calls heartily, and strides away.

I glance over my shoulder and observe that Jeanie is hanging back with Sandy, so I start along beside Tammie. The crowd, so still and silent while we were driving, pushes eagerly forward. Something of their tense interest in the sport gets to me and thrills me with an interest all my own. For the first time since the match was made, I have a feeling that, no matter the outcome, I am going to enjoy it.

The first hole is a matter of three hundred and fifty yards to a slightly elevated green deeply trapped on both sides, but open to a straight approach. From his position, Mr. McPherson has to resort to a brassie. He gets the shot away clean, but again it is pulled and leaves him with a bunker yet to be negotiated.

Judging my distance, I would have taken a mid-iron, or at least a number three. Tammie hands me a mashie, and I do not dispute him.

"Anither ane easy," he mutters. "Ye wullna mak' th' green. Play fer th' spat atween th' twa traps."

I am a little short, but the broad green is straight before me. Mr. McPherson clears the trap nicely, but his shot is a bit hard and fetches up in the long grass across the green, narrowly missing the opposite bunker.

"Tak yer time; tak yer time, laddie," Tammie exhorts me, as I reach for the mashie niblick which he holds on to and thrusts the mashie into my hands instead. "Ye're safer wi' this ane; but hauld yer een on th' ba' till I tell ye ye can leuk up."

The advice is most timely. At once I am aware that I was on the point of hurrying to play the ball up as quickly as I could. Now I leisurely take a firm stance, glance slowly to the flag, which I can see over the high edge of the green, and determinedly keep my eyes on the ball as I take an easy stroke. When I climb up to the green, I find my ball only four feet short of the hole. I win this first one, actually in a par four to Mr. McPherson's six.

Jean and Sandy are still back with the crowd, and as I walk toward the next tee I review this, my first, accomplishment. It is borne in upon me that by following Tammie's every word to the letter, notwithstanding the measure of luck which I frankly feel attended my efforts, nevertheless I made every stroke correctly.

He did not tell me to play too slowly or too carefully. In fact the total of his advice could be summed up in the insistence that I should play well within my power. I keep this constantly in mind as we halve the next two holes.

On the rather long fourth, Mr. McPherson's two shots chance to go straight and land him on the green. I say chance because with the power he gives to them, he is quite apt to pull, and even to slice. My third is a little short, and he is down while I still have to putt the odd.

The fifth goes very badly for me and for a while I am quite in despair. Following his long drive, which again is happily in the fairway, unconsciously I yield to the impulse to equal it. As a result, my shoulders and body go into the stroke, and my ball slices into the rough at the right. This lapse and return to my old fault, which I have vainly hoped was forever behind me, perturb me greatly. In spite of Tammie's urgent plea to play easily and make certain only to get out, again I give too much effort with the iron, and still lie in the rough. When we reach the green with three strokes worse I ruefully pick up my ball.

The loss of the hole and the possible loss of the match disturb me far less than the thought that all this instruction and all my care have gone for naught. It seems to me in that moment that I am condemned always to remain the duffer. I know how the stroke should be correctly played, but something in my temperament, perhaps, is defeating me. The reflection is very bitter.

I try, however, to master myself, and listen earnestly to Tammie's advice; yet on the next I make only one creditable shot and lose again to the genial minister's steady five. Then, as I walk toward the tee, endeavoring not to appear as disconsolate as I am feeling, Jeanie brushes past me.

"Don't take it all so seriously, Bobbie," she whispers. "I am thinking—of something that makes all this seem of no importance at all." She turns away and is gone before I can reply.

Up to the last two holes I have thought that Tammie's advice was everything helpful, but it seems as nothing now. Gone on the instant is my ill feeling toward myself. Light-heartedness and confidence even come back to me. I go forward eagerly.

I do not watch Mr. McPherson's drive and have not the least idea where his ball lands. And what is far more important, I do not in the least care. I concentrate my thought on my hands and arms, and take a slow practice swing before driving.

My drive, while not long, is straight, the stroke is correctly made and I have felt altogether in control

[230]

of the moderate effort given to it. That I halve this hole is due more to Mr. McPherson's inability to control the long shots he almost invariably gets away than to the effectiveness of my own strokes, for at this moment I am concerned not at all with their number and only with getting back on my game.

And right here I make an interesting discovery. In my determination not to overplay my strokes, I find that it is almost, although not quite, as harmful to try to swing too easily. Evidently for each individual player there is an even measure of power and speed, with proper rhythm, that cannot be stressed in either direction to advantage.

As I go on, concentrating solely upon each shot as it comes up and with a nonchalance—thanks to Jeanie—toward the final result that is not feigned, my game becomes almost automatically steady, and well within myself I halve the following holes to the turn. And I learn further that once my stroke is started properly, I can give increasingly more power to my arms and wrists without disaster.

That I am two down at this point, frankly, does not bother me a whit. I am finding a heretofore unknown enjoyment in which worry, nervousness and uncertainty have no place at all. On the other hand, despite his advantage, my increasing steadiness seems to urge my very friendly opponent to greater and even greater effort.

Distance is generally his portion, but not direction, and more often now he plays the odd after our drives and right up to the greens. Miraculous as it appears to me when later I consider it, I go into the lead, and on the seventeenth Mr. McPherson picks up his ball and congratulates me without the slightest evidence of chagrin.

And as if this act is the signal to relieve the ardent followers of this modest match from their bondage of silence and unfailing orderliness, a great shout rends the air; they come streaming across green and fairway to surround us and to contribute their comments on the play and the outcome.

Caustic, and at times barbed, repartee is tossed back and forth between loser and winner until it seems that scarcely a person there but who had something on it, with its inheritance of joy or chagrin. Mr. McPherson comes in for much frank chaffing to all of which he responds with unruffled good nature. A few, like Tammie, Jamie and the burly smith, crowd up to shake my hand or treat me to a wholesome whack on the back; but rather curiously, as it first appears to me, the real ovation is for Sandy Macgregor and his triumph.

I do not get this at once; I am a little embarrassed, considerably dazed and altogether too gratified to view the matter impersonally. But the remarks I overhear all about me do not leave me long in doubt.

And truly, as I see it now, all credit is due the canny old teacher.

To take such a hopeless duffer as was I when I first came to him, and within the space of a few weeks send him to victory against such a seasoned player as the clergyman is a rare achievement. That I was, fortunately, a creditable exponent of his instructing skill is glory enough for me and assuredly all that I deserve.

This match crystallizes my understanding of many points of play. First, it is almost shocking to realize, as I do now, how very much one's state of mind has to do with the quality of his game. Again, barring what we prefer to term luck and the breaks, let us grant that every player has his respective standard. Even under stress, one cannot expect to go vastly beyond that standard, although in critical moments one feels the well nigh irresistible impulse to attempt it. The matter of importance, however, is to maintain that standard, which demands sole attention upon the shot at hand and its execution with a fine balance of moderation and assurance.

From my opponent I draw a lesson in another way. Mr. McPherson has a splendid temperament for play. He is very powerful, and one readily sees that his mental direction is to unleash that power upon his stroke. Sandy explains the matter a bit differently; but I should say that this genial clergyman gives all his muscles to power and none whatsoever to guidance.

We are at dinner, the four of us, and by all odds the jolliest in point of exuberance is the genial minister. I have never seen him in a mood of such rollicking fun. By common consent, on Jeanie's suggestion, we are celebrating in ale alone, and in truth there is no lack of it.

The dinner itself is one to remember, and I shall not soon forget it. It is simple, perhaps, but deliciously tasty and wholesome, and marvelously prepared even to the luscious pheasant done to the exact turn.

This dinner, by the way, is being given at the Manse. That is the fact; but even now I am hardly able to comprehend how possibly I could have come in the winner—and by two holes at that.

It may have been due to the influence of Sandy's watchful presence, who was ever a little away, never within speaking distance of me, but whose keen eyes did not miss one stroke.

Or it might have been because of little old Tammie's unruffled temperament and constant encouragement, to "Keep your ee on th' ba', laddie. Ne'er mind what th' minister's daein'. Mak your ain stroke; ye can dae it. Be cauld, man; be cauld. Ah, that was a recht bonnie ane!"

But I shall always believe that it was chiefly due

[234]

to Jeanie's inspiration, her unfailing faith and confidence in me—and lastly to the fact that upon her suggestion I became not entirely concerned with the match, to the exclusion of a frequent thought of another event of vastly more importance, that stood only a short while before me.

As for Mr. McPherson's side of it, he finally divulges his "secret." He declares that he was so afraid he would be denied his pheasant, because of my great absent-mindedness which he had observed of late, he ordered them several days in advance, and, once committed, could not possibly come out the victor.

At this, Jeanie laughs delightedly and says that when she went to fetch them, Wullie Burnside seemed to have forgotten all about any previous arrangement.

The days slip by rapidly. I make all I can of my shortening opportunities with Sandy, although, I must admit, my mind is not entirely occupied with its earlier thoughtful consideration of the stroke.

We are married at the Manse, quietly, and I daresay thoroughly. There is a reception afterward on the lawn, and I am convinced that the whole of Elie is there, with the single exception of Sandy Macgregor whom I do not see at all.

For the occasion, I have set up a credit at the tap in the Inn, a most fortunate idea; for presently we are relieved of the most of our guests and can prepare for our early departure. Mr. and Mrs. McPherson are motoring with us to Edinburra and will dine with us before returning. . . . It is almost time to leave.

I hurry over to the Inn to say good-by to Bob Ferguson. My bags have been sent on, but I go up to my room for a last look around. It is quite likely that I may have forgotten something. As I enter, the first thing that meets my eyes is a golf bag. Now I am certain I had not overlooked that, for I distinctly remember locking it.

Wonderingly I take out the driver. It is a sweet club, perfectly matched to me.

Comprehension dawns upon me. I snatch up the bag and dash over to the Manse. One after the other, I show the full set to Jean. Together we hurry along the path and up the little hill to Sandy's cottage. Tammie, the caddie, is there alone. To my excited question, he tells us, with a shrewd smile, that "Sandy has gaen feshin'." And there is nothing we can do about it. To leave any payment or gift of money is unthinkable.

* * *

We prolong our honeymoon trip and arrive home too late for the club championship at Folothru. However, Jeanie and I enter the mixed Scottish four-somes, which, due to Jeanie's marvelous playing, we win quite handily. In the finals, as Dick Hilton picks up his ball on the fifteenth and we start to cut across to the club-house, Angelica looks long at the club champion, and by virtue of that, her newly acquired husband.

"Dickie," she drawls, "thank God Bobbie didn't get back in time for the championship."

"Yes," Jeanie says instantly, "I am sure we can all be duly thankful for that."

As Jarvis drives us home, we laugh heartily over this first sign of irritation I have ever observed my dear wife to show.